Savor the Flavor

101 DELICIOUS EASY-TO-PREPARE
LOW-FAT RECIPES

Gail L. Becker, R.D.

WINGS BOOKS

New York • Avenel, New Jersey

This 1994 edition is published by Wings Books, distributed by Random House Value Publishing, Inc., 40 Engelhard Avenue, Avenel, New Jersey 07001, by arrangement with Gail Becker Associates, Inc.

Random House
New York • Toronto • London • Sydney • Auckland

Printed and bound in the United States of America
Printed on recycled paper

Library of Congress Cataloging-in-Publication Data

Becker, Gail L.
Savor the flavor / by Gail Becker.
p.   cm.
Originally published: Elmsford, N.Y. :Benjamin Co., 1981.
Includes index.
ISBN 0-517-10026-6
1. Low-calorie diet—Recipes.   2. Low-cholesterol diet—Recipes.
3. Sugar-free diet—Recipes.   4. Salt-free diet—Recipes.
5. Food substitutes.   I. Title.
RM222.2.B398   1994
641.5′63—dc20   93-32575
                                                           CIP

8 7 6 5 4 3 2 1

About the Author

Gail L. Becker, a registered dietitian, is a graduate of Drexel University. She has managed the food and nutrition department of the world's largest weight-control organization, directed dietetics at a large metropolitan hospital, and headed dietetic services for a major food company.

Ms. Becker is a member of the American Dietetics Association, the Society for Nutrition Education, the American College of Nutrition, the Institute of Technology, the American Home Economics Association, and many other professional organizations. She conducts nutrition seminars and appears frequently on television and radio programs as an authority on nutrition. Her articles have been published in leading national publications.

Ms. Becker is the president of a Great Neck, New York–based communications company serving the food, nutrition, and health promotion industries.

Acknowledgments

I would like to thank Michele J. Lambrech; Daphne Philippides; Annette R. Schottenfeld, M.B.A., R.D.; Francine M. Scuderi; and Elizabeth Hanna Thomas for their contributions to the preparation of this book.

Acknowledgments would not be complete without a special thanks to Ben Eisenstadt, Marvin Eisenstadt, Jeffrey Eisenstadt, and Barbara Eisenstadt for their special commitment to making this book possible.

Dear Friend,

Developing good eating habits is an important step toward good health, but at Cumberland we understand that "good eating" is so much more than choosing foods that are low in fat and calories.

The joy of hearty cuisine lies in its rich aromas, delicious flavors, and mouthwatering presentation. Therefore, the secret to enjoying nutritious food is discovering alternative ways of preparing old favorites by substituting healthier ingredients and seasonings. Very simply, that's what this cookbook is all about. Since people have different taste preferences, we've offered a wide selection of recipes, making it easy to create varied menus to appeal to everyone's appetite.

We hope you enjoy the recipes in *Savor the Flavor,* which use many Cumberland products to help keep fat and calorie contents low without sacrificing taste. If you have any questions, comments, or suggestions about these products, please write to us at the following address: Cumberland Packing Corp., P.O. Box 140, Dept. STF, Great Neck, NY 11021. We'd love to hear from you!

Sincerely,

Gail L. Becker, R.D.
Nutrition Consultant
Cumberland Packing Corp.

Contents

Introduction

Dietary Guidelines for Americans: Would the Real Rules Please Stand Up?

"High-Fat Diet Linked to Greater Risk of Chronic Illness"

"Study Fails to Link Dietary Fat and Cancer"

"Fruits and Veggies, Yes, but Easy on the Alcohol"

"Cancer and Coffee Not Linked, Study Says"

What's going on? Is the expert advice in the media fact or fiction? Do headlines like these make you want to head to the library to conduct your own dietary research? Or do they make you want to throw your hands up and head for the nearest fast-food joint?

If you're like most Americans, you've probably done both. It's not surprising we're confused by reports offering dietary advice. In a world where today's miracle cure is often tomorrow's hype, it's difficult to know what to believe, much less what to eat! The truth is, it's easier to navigate through the myriad of dietary advice when you have a little basic knowledge about nutrition.

In 1980 the U.S. Department of Agriculture (USDA) and the U.S. Department of Health and Human Services (USDHHS) jointly published the initial Dietary Guidelines for Americans in response to the need for authoritative, consistent guidelines on diet and health. Since then, these guidelines have been reviewed and twice updated by two federal advisory panels of nutrition experts.

The third and most recent edition of these guidelines, issued in 1990, emphasizes maintenance of healthy body weight and limiting intake of fat and saturated fat. Many of these seven guidelines directly correspond with the USDA's food guide, represented by a pyramid graphic. By reviewing the following dietary guidelines, you will learn how they can promote good health.

1. **EAT A VARIETY OF FOODS.** Variety is not only the spice of life—it's also the best way to ensure adequate intake of the many nutrients necessary for good health. Only a well-balanced diet that includes foods from the five food groups can provide you with all the calories, vitamins, minerals, and other nutrients that play crucial roles in promoting good health.

   In the past, before many foods were enriched or fortified, people were more concerned with deficiency diseases, such as scurvy. Ironically, many of the chronic diseases and illnesses that plague us today—cancer, heart disease, and high blood pressure, in particular—may be attributed to an *overabundance* of certain compounds in the diet. Of particular concern is the role of dietary fat in the development of many chronic diseases.

   Due to the varying chemical composition of these compounds, the human body utilizes carbohydrates most efficiently, followed by proteins, and then fats. However, all three compounds are necessary for good health. The solution is to eat sensible quantities of different types of food.

2. **MAINTAIN IDEAL WEIGHT.** There's a difference between being overweight and overfat. Two people of identical height and weight with different bone and muscle structure and percentage of body fat will have radically different appearances. This is because muscle weighs almost three times as much as fat. The following chart of suggested body weights for men and women are appropriate guidelines for most healthy adults. Refer to the chart to determine if you're within the suggested range for your height.

Suggested Weights for Adults

Height[1]	Weight in pounds[2]	
	19 to 34 years	**35 years and over**
5'0"	[3]97–128	108–138
5'1"	101–132	111–143
5'2"	104–137	115–148
5'3"	107–141	119–152
5'4"	111–146	122–157
5'5"	114–150	126–162
5'6"	118–155	130–167
5'7"	121–160	134–172
5'8"	125–164	138–178
5'9"	129–169	142–183
5'10"	132–174	146–188
5'11"	136–179	151–194
6'0"	140–184	155–199
6'1"	144–189	159–205
6'2"	148–195	164–210
6'3"	152–200	168–216
6'4"	156–205	173–222
6'5"	160–211	177–228
6'6"	164–216	182–234

[1] Without shoes

[2] Without clothes

[3] The higher weights in the ranges generally apply to men, who tend to have more muscle and bone; the lower weights more often apply to women, who tend to have less muscle and bone.

SOURCE: Derived from National Research Council, 1989.

Many health experts agree that combining a balanced diet that is low in fat with regular exercise is the key to good health and weight control. Studies show that women, and men and women over the age of 50, generally pay greater attention to nutritional recommendations but do not exercise strenuously, while younger people, and men in particular, are more prone to rigorous exercise without adhering to good nutrition habits. Break these trends and make every effort to include both in your lifestyle.

One guaranteed result of regular exercise is an increased metabolism, or ability to burn calories. This effect lasts even after actual exercise has stopped. You'll also tone muscle, improve cardiovascular conditioning, increase flexibility, and enjoy a sleeker silhouette. If you maintain your intake of calories while increasing the amount of calories you burn through exercise, you will lose weight.

You can avoid the "have to" mind-set and experience greater success if you make exercising an activity you enjoy. Before you think, "But I don't have time to exercise!" say to yourself, "Yes, I do." Walking the dog, washing the car, mowing the lawn . . . anything that gets you moving is exercise—and good for you! Trick yourself into exercising by getting off the bus one stop early, taking stairs instead of elevators, or doing light stretches while watching TV.

Regardless of your age, even moderate exercise provides many of the same health benefits as more strenuous activities. The following chart of calories burned while performing common activities may surprise and motivate you to include more of these activities in your day.

Approximate Energy Expenditures
(150-Pound Person in Various Activities)

ACTIVITY	CALORIES PER HOUR
Lying down or sleeping	80
Sitting	100
Driving an automobile	120
Standing	140

Domestic work	180
Walking, 2-1/2 mph	210
Bicycling, 5-1/2 mph	210
Gardening	220
Golf; lawn mowing, power mower	250
Bowling	270
Walking, 3-3/4 mph	300
Swimming, 1/4 mph	300
Square dancing, volleyball, roller skating	350
Tennis	420
Skiing, 10 mph	600
Squash or handball	600
Bicycling, 13 mph	660
Running, 10 mph	900

SOURCE: Based on material prepared by Robert E. Johnson, M.D., Ph.D., and colleagues, University of Illinois.

3. **AVOID TOO MUCH FAT, SATURATED FAT, AND CHOLES-TEROL.** The typical American diet remains high in fat and cholesterol. Fats, which are combinations of different compounds called fatty acids, are generally classified as saturated, monounsaturated, and polyunsaturated, depending upon the main type of fatty acid they contain.

Dietary fats that are mostly composed of saturated fatty acids are considered the most dangerous to good health, as they have been linked to elevated blood cholesterol levels. Animal foods, such as meat, poultry, whole milk, eggs, cheese, and butter, along with coconut and palm oils are the primary culprits and sources of saturated fat in the United States.

Cholesterol, a waxy substance found in cell membranes, is vital for life. Substances called lipoproteins are the carriers of cholesterol within the body. Low-density lipoproteins, or LDLs, transport blood cholesterol from the liver to other parts of the body for use. Extra cholesterol remaining in the bloodstream collects along blood vessel walls, a condition known as atherosclerosis. Because this condition blocks the flow of blood to major arteries, LDLs are frequently termed "bad cholesterol."

High-density lipoproteins, or HDLs, are responsible for returning cholesterol to the liver for processing or removal from the body. Since HDLs remove excess cholesterol from the blood and prevent accumulation along the arteries, HDLs are referred to as "good cholesterol."

LDLs and HDLs contribute to your total cholesterol level. A desirable level for total blood cholesterol is 200 mg/dL or less, with an LDL cholesterol level of 130 mg/dL or less. A total blood cholesterol level of 240 mg/dL or greater is considered "high" blood cholesterol, but any level above 200 mg/dL increases your risk for coronary heart disease.

It is estimated that more than half of all American adults fall into this category. For most people, diet and exercise are clear factors in controlling high blood cholesterol. Other factors, including gender, hereditary, blood pressure, and smoking, can also determine your risk for heart disease.

Some studies report that moderate amounts of many monounsaturated and polyunsaturated fats have been shown to lower blood cholesterol levels when used in place of saturated fat. These types of fats, which include margarine and vegetable, peanut, olive, and canola oils, should still be eaten in moderation. Remember, all fats provide 9 calories per gram—more than double the calories provided by one gram of carbohydrate (4 calories) or protein (4 calories) —and should be limited in the diet.

Although the American Heart Association and other health experts recommend that people consume no more than 30 percent of their calories from fat, most Americans tend to eat more, around 45 percent. Identify low-fat foods by referring to the product's label to determine what percent of your daily fat allotment a serving contributes.

In general, there are no "good" foods or "bad" foods. What's good or bad is the amount of or frequency with which you choose to consume certain foods. An egg for breakfast once or twice a week may be acceptable; eggs for breakfast four or five days a week isn't! Here are a few additional tips for limiting fat intake:

- Choose lean meat, fish, poultry, dry beans, and peas as protein sources.
- Trim excess fat from meat before cooking. Bake, broil, grill, microwave, or boil rather than fry.
- Consume eggs and organ meats in moderation, as these are very high in cholesterol.
- Limit your consumption of butter, creamy sauces, shortenings, palm oil, and coconut oil, as well as food made with these products.
- Read labels carefully to find hidden fats in foods.

4. **EAT FOODS WITH ADEQUATE STARCH AND FIBER.** Carbohydrates and fats are the top sources of energy in the average U.S. citizen's diet. One gram of carbohydrate provides 4 calories, which, as previously mentioned, is less than half the calories contained in one gram of fat. Therefore, you can eat greater quantities of carbohydrate-rich food for the same amount of calories as a smaller portion of fatty food.

Simple carbohydrates, also known as sugars, are found naturally in fruit and other whole foods, such as sugarcane, beets, and corn. Most or all of their dietary fiber and nutrients are stripped away in the refinement process. Therefore, sugars provide "empty" calories with no real nutritional value.

Complex carbohydrates are chains of simple sugars found naturally in grains, legumes, vegetables, and fruits. Rich in essential vitamins, minerals, and dietary fiber, complex carbohydrates are stored as starch and must be broken down into simple carbohydrates to be absorbed by the body. As a result, complex carbohydrates supply calories at a much slower, steadier rate than sugar.

Dietary fiber is critical for good health maintenance. Low-fiber diets have been associated with higher incidence of certain types of cancer. By increasing your consumption of complex carbohydrates, which have high levels of dietary fiber, you may reduce the symptoms of chronic constipation, diverticulosis, and irritable bowel syndrome. Fiber also provides bulk and texture, allowing you to eat less and still feel full.

In the past, weight-conscious people were told to shun "starchy" foods, such as potatoes, rice, and bread. Ironically, these were often replaced with high-fat foods: Consider the traditional "diet plate" of a hamburger without the bun, served with creamy cottage cheese. Today, realizing that carbohydrates should constitute a large portion of our diet, it would be wiser to request the entire bun and opt for a small low-fat beef or turkey burger with a generous serving of fresh vegetables. Or you might have a taste for something entirely different: a large leafy salad with water-packed tuna or perhaps a colorful fruit plate with low-fat cheese. Remember, variety is the key!

Here are other tips to increase your complex carbohydrate intake:

- Add legumes such as peas, lentils, kidney beans, and garbanzo beans to soups, salads, and main dishes.
- Choose more whole grain or bran breads, rolls, and cereals instead of white flour bread and sugary cereals. Limit intake of high-fat selections, such as croissants and muffins.
- Substitute brown rice for white rice.
- When possible, substitute all or part whole grain flour for enriched white flour.
- Eat whole fruits and vegetables raw or keep cooking to a minimum to retain the maximum amount of nutrients. If you drink fruit or vegetable juices, look for brands that still contain fiber (pulp).

5. **AVOID TOO MUCH SUGAR.** The average American consumes more than 130 pounds of sugar a year. Surveys show that while concern over fat consumption is rising, actual consumption of sweets is rising as well. Although there is no compelling evidence linking sugar to health problems such as heart attacks or blood vessel diseases, remember that sugar is a source of empty calories. And many of us have firsthand experience with a major hazard of too much sugar: tooth decay.

Also known as dental caries, tooth decay poses a greater risk to people who eat sweets frequently. If you snack between meals, the sugary residue left on your teeth is potentially damaging. Be especially careful after eating chewy sweets like gum, caramels, or dried fruit.

In addition to obvious sources such as candy or jelly, other foods that aren't considered "sweets," such as ketchup, may be high in sugar, too. Many foods that naturally contain sugar, such as fruit and milk, are preferable, as they are also good sources of other nutrients.

People with diabetes must monitor their intake of all sugars very carefully, although the disease is not caused by excessive sugar intake, as was once thought. Individuals with type II diabetes (also known as non-insulin-dependent diabetes) can often greatly improve their health status and slow down the progression of the disease with a diet high in dietary fiber and low in sugar, fat, and calories.

Limiting your sugar intake can help you maintain a healthy weight. To trim excess sugar from your diet, you can:

- Use less of all sugars, including white sugar, brown sugar, honey, molasses, and syrup.
- Limit consumption of sugary foods such as soft drinks, ice cream, candy, cakes, and cookies, many of which may also be high in fat.
- Eat more whole fruits, which contain natural sugars as well as nutrients and provide energy to the body at a slower, more consistent rate. Fruits canned without sugar or in light syrup are also good choices.
- Scan food labels for "code names" for different forms of sugar used in many processed foods: sucrose, glucose, lactose, fructose, maltose, and syrups.
- Replace a portion of the sugar in baked goods with a heat-stable sugar substitute such as Sweet 'N Low® or Sweet One®.

6. **AVOID TOO MUCH SODIUM.** Table salt contains sodium and chloride, two essential minerals needed for proper fluid balance and nervous system maintenance. Sodium is found in many popular foods such as soft drinks, processed foods, condiments, sauces, pickled items, salty snacks, and sandwich meats. To meet the daily sodium requirement recommended for adults by most health profes-

sionals—less than 2,400 mg—you'd most likely never have to pick up the salt shaker. Many people already consume far more than necessary.

High blood pressure, a dangerous health condition that affects about 1 in 3 Americans and is one of the leading risk factors for coronary heart disease, may often be controlled through diet modification. Studies have shown that when people who are sodium sensitive restrict their intake of sodium, their blood pressure drops.

While high blood pressure is linked to a variety of factors, including heredity, obesity, and excessive consumption of alcohol, it is still difficult to predict who will develop the condition. Most people can benefit to some extent by limiting sodium consumption.

To avoid too much sodium, you can:

- Omit added salt in cooking and on the table.
- Flavor food with herbs, spices, citrus fruits, and flavored vinegars.
- Limit intake of salty snacks such as potato chips, pretzels, salted nuts, popcorn, cheese, pickled foods, cured meats, and condiments.

7. **IF YOU DRINK ALCOHOL, DO SO IN MODERATION.** Moderate drinking is generally classified as no more than 1 drink a day for women and no more than 2 drinks a day for men. If you are weight conscious, keep in mind that alcohol is high in calories and low in nutrients.

Vitamin and mineral deficiencies are common in heavy drinkers, who may lose their appetite and consume inadequate amounts of nutrients. Additionally, the body's ability to absorb and utilize available nutrients is adversely affected by alcohol. The body's ability to burn fat is also hampered, although alcohol itself contains no fat.

Always be skeptical when assessing the true health benefits of studies with findings that sound too good to be true. For example, a news report in the early 1990s purported that the French were less likely to die from heart disease than were Americans, a finding supposedly related to the Europeans' drinking moderate amounts of red wine. However, a wide variety of other factors could have also contributed to this lower rate of heart disease. The report certainly made no mention of the increased risk of high blood pressure, certain types of cancer, hemorrhagic stroke, cirrhosis of the liver, inflammation of the pancreas, neurological disorders, and damage to the brain also associated with drinking.

Alcohol consumption can be hazardous to both your short- and long-term health. Very moderate or no consumption at all is strongly encouraged for women who are pregnant or trying to conceive, as severe birth defects have been linked to the use of alcohol by the mother. It is strongly recommended that people in the categories below also abstain entirely:

- Individuals who plan to engage in activities requiring skill and attention, such as driving.
- Individuals taking medication, which may increase blood alcohol levels or alcohol's negative effect on the brain (alcohol may also affect the toxicity of the medication).
- Children and adolescents.
- Individuals who cannot control their drinking.

Pyramid Power for Good Health

The concept of eating sensible amounts of different types of foods for good health sounds simple enough. But how much of what types of food? If you are part of the generation accustomed to partaking of equal quantities from the "four food groups"—bread, milk, meat, and fruits and vegetables—you may be wondering what goes where.

In an effort to end consumer confusion, the USDA proposed an updated graphic, the Food Guide Pyramid, to teach people how much and what types of food they should eat to strive for good health. After much debate, a pyramid shape was selected to demonstrate desirable quantities of various food categories.

The lowest and largest pyramid tier represents 6 to 11 recommended servings per day of complex carbohydrates, which include breads, grains, cereals, and pasta. If this sounds like a lot, keep in mind that one serving equals one slice of bread, one ounce of ready-to-eat cereal, or a half cup of cooked cereal, rice, or pasta.

The second tier represents 5 to 9 recommended servings per day of

Food Guide Pyramid
A Guide to Daily Food Choices

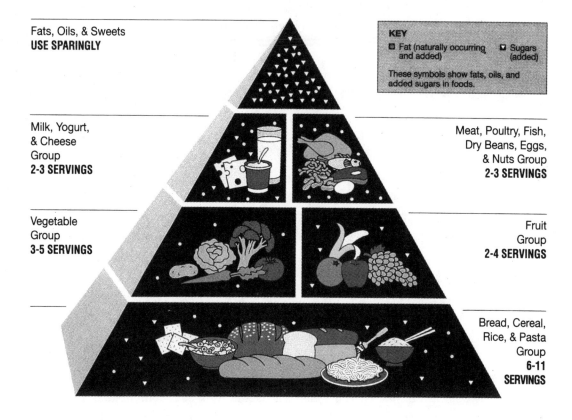

Fats, Oils, & Sweets
USE SPARINGLY

KEY
- Fat (naturally occurring and added)
- Sugars (added)

These symbols show fats, oils, and added sugars in foods.

Milk, Yogurt, & Cheese Group
2-3 SERVINGS

Meat, Poultry, Fish, Dry Beans, Eggs, & Nuts Group
2-3 SERVINGS

Vegetable Group
3-5 SERVINGS

Fruit Group
2-4 SERVINGS

Bread, Cereal, Rice, & Pasta Group
6-11 SERVINGS

SOURCE: U.S. Department of Agriculture/U.S. Department of Health and Human Services

fruits and vegetables. Fruits and vegetables are excellent choices for people concerned with weight control. In general, these foods are low in calories, have a high dietary fiber and water content, and are rich in vitamins and minerals. Recent studies have also established a link between high intake of certain vitamins and a diminished risk of certain types of chronic diseases. One serving is considered one medium-size whole fruit, one cup leafy raw vegetables, or one half cup canned, cooked, or chopped fruit or vegetables.

The third tier represents 2 to 3 servings of meat or other protein-rich foods and 2 to 3 servings of cheese or dairy products. One serving of meat is 3 ounces cooked, roughly the size of a deck of cards; as a meat alternative, one half cup of cooked dry beans, one egg, or two tablespoons of peanut butter provides an equal amount of protein. One serving of dairy could be a one-ounce slice of cheese or one cup of yogurt or milk. Plan meals with smaller portions of these foods and with larger quantities of grains and vegetables. Aim for healthier selections, such as poultry without the skin, lean cuts of beef and pork, skim milk, and reduced-fat dairy products.

The tip of the pyramid represents fats, oils, and sweets. Even these "forbidden" foods can be a part of a balanced diet, but they should be eaten sparingly.

The Food Label Link

To help you select foods that meet the recommendations of the Dietary Guidelines and the Food Guide Pyramid, the Food and Drug Administration (FDA) and the USDA now require that all food products be labeled with specific nutrient information. The new food labels help you monitor the amount of fat, saturated fat, cholesterol, and sodium in the food by placing descriptors, such as "low," "reduced," or "free," on the front. Other descriptors help you identify good sources of dietary fiber, vitamins, and minerals, with terms such as "high in" and "good source of."

Additionally, certain claims about the relationship between a food or nutrient and the risk of a disease or health-related condition may also

Serving size in both household and metric units. All manufacturers are required to use the same standard serving sizes.

The number of servings per container.

Total calories per serving amount.

Nutrition panel heading.

Nutrition information per serving amount.

The rounded number of calories from fat. (Grams of fat x 9 calories per gram of fat.)

Percent Daily Value (or % DV) shows how a food fits into the overall daily diet. It represents the percent of suggested daily nutrients each serving provides.

Reference values based on calorie needs. May vary based on your needs.

Caloric value of the three energy-producing nutrients.

Nutrition Facts

Serving Size 1/2 cup (114g)
Servings Per Container 4

Amount Per Serving

Calories 90   Calories from Fat 30

                           % Daily Value*

Total Fat 3g	**5%**
Saturated Fat 0g	**0%**
Cholesterol 0mg	**0%**
Sodium 300mg	**13%**
Total Carbohydrate 13g	**4%**
Dietary Fiber 3g	**12%**
Sugars 3g	
Protein 3g	

Vitamin A	80%	Vitamin C	60%
Calcium	4%	Iron	4%

* Percent Daily Values are based on a 2,000 calorie diet. Your daily values may be higher or lower depending on your calorie needs:

	Calories	2,000	2,500
Total Fat	Less than	65g	80g
Sat Fat	Less than	20g	25g
Cholesterol	Less than	300mg	300mg
Sodium	Less than	2,400mg	2,400mg
Total Carbohydrate		300g	375g
Fiber		25g	30g

Calories per gram:
Fat 9   •   Carbohydrate 4   •   Protein 4

appear on the front of the label. Health claims that have been approved include:

- calcium and a reduced risk of osteoporosis;
- sodium and an increased risk of hypertension;
- dietary saturated fat and cholesterol and an increased risk of heart disease;
- dietary fat and an increased risk of cancer;
- fiber-containing grain products, fruits, and vegetables and a reduced risk of cancer;
- fiber-containing (particularly soluble fiber) grain products, fruits, and vegetables and a reduced risk of heart disease;
- fruits and vegetables and a reduced risk of cancer.

However, you do not have to select only foods with descriptors or health claims to follow the dietary recommendations. In moderation, all foods can fit into a healthy diet.

The back of the new food label also provides valuable information. The nutrition panel, now titled "Nutrition Facts," has a standard format that helps make comparing food products easier. To understand how to read the Nutrition Facts panel, refer to the sample label shown.

Reading food labels can be fun! After a few excursions to the grocery store, you'll become expert at which foods to include in a healthful diet.

How to Use This Book

Now that you know the facts, the question still remains: "What do I eat?"

Let's face it: Eating involves a lot more than merely satisfying nutrient needs. Every meal—whether it's a leisurely breakfast, tailgate lunch, or buffet dinner party—should be a delicious, satisfying experience. We want our food to burst with fabulous flavor. We want a spectacular presentation when it's served on the table. We want to cook and bake with healthful ingredients that are easy to find, use, and store. And of course, we want to prepare our meals as quickly as possible—all the more time to enjoy them!

Our homemade creations should look like they arrived from a gourmet restaurant, even when we've prepared something as simple as roasted chicken breast. Ideally, these memorable meals should also be low in fat and calories and use a variety of nutritious ingredients. That is what this book is all about.

We'll teach you how to prepare mouthwatering recipes that are easily incorporated into a healthful diet. We've included a variety of widely available ingredients and kept preparation time brief. Most recipes derive only 30 percent or less of their calories from fat, which is the percentage recommended by most health experts.

With the Food Guide Pyramid in mind, our recipes include plenty of fruits, vegetables, and grains and use smaller quantities of higher-fat meat, cheese, and dairy products. Recipes are marked with symbols indicating where they fall in the pyramid. Remember, symbols appear only for the predominant food categories in the recipe. The recipe may still contain a smaller amount of other food categories that can add up when looking at your complete diet.

To make eating healthy even tastier, Sweet 'N Low® granulated sugar substitute and Butter Buds® all-natural butter-flavored granules have been used to replace a portion of the sugar and fat in these recipes. They are breakthrough products for people who have chosen low-calorie, low-fat dietary habits. Both are excellent for tabletop flavoring use and are well suited for use in cooking and baking, retaining their flavor under high temperatures. For people with different tastes, Sweet One® granulated sugar substitute may be used in place of equivalent amounts of Sweet 'N Low with no change in results.

The menu suggestions in our final chapter provide tasty, appealing ideas for such occasions as a Best Ever Brunch, Cocktail Party, Holiday Dinner, Perfect Picnic, and Western Barbecue. We hope these ideas will encourage you to center all your healthy feasts around the nutritious foods used in these recipes. Enjoy!

Key to the Symbols

 — **Dairy**

 — **Bread**

 — **Fruit**

 — **Vegetable**

 — **Meat**

B
B — **Butter Buds**®

 — **Sweet 'N Low**®

Weights and Measures Equivalencies

Dash = less than 1/8 teaspoon

3 teaspoons = 1 tablespoon = 1/2 fluid ounce

2 tablespoons = 1/8 cup = 1 fluid ounce

4 tablespoons = 1/4 cup = 2 fluid ounces

8 tablespoons = 1/2 cup = 4 fluid ounces

12 tablespoons = 3/4 cup = 6 fluid ounces

16 tablespoons = 1 cup = 8 fluid ounces

2 cups = 1 pint

2 pints = 1 quart

4 quarts = 1 gallon

1 ounce = 28 grams

16 ounces = 1 pound

About the Products

Butter Buds®

When trying to limit your intake of calories and cholesterol—and who isn't these days?—Butter Buds® all-natural butter-flavored granules are the ideal substitution for butter or margarine. Sold in major supermarkets, Butter Buds® are available in three forms: granulated Sprinkles, packaged in 2.5-ounce canisters; a granulated Mix that can be reconstituted with water to form a hot, buttery liquid, packaged in boxes of eight 1/2-ounce envelopes;

and a Spread (currently available in select markets), sold in 1-pound packages of 4 sticks or 2 tubs.

Butter Buds® Sprinkles and Mix are 100 percent fat- and cholesterol-free. The amount of flavor in 1 tablespoon of Butter Buds® is equivalent to 1 tablespoon of butter or margarine. One serving of Sprinkles (1 teaspoon) contains 5 calories, and one serving of Mix (1 teaspoon) contains 5 calories. Butter Buds®' delicious natural flavor is extracted from the oils in real butter and dried to a powderlike form, leaving the fat and calories behind. This process is terrific news for health-conscious people who love the taste of butter.

One serving of Butter Buds® Spread (1 tablespoon) contains 25 calories, 2.6 grams of fat, and no cholesterol. While regular margarine and vegetable oils are cholesterol-free, they still contain between 100 and 120 calories each per tablespoon, the same amount as butter. All Butter Buds® varieties are also comparable to or lower than butter or margarine in sodium content, containing about 70 milligrams per serving.

Butter Buds® Sprinkles, Mix, and Spread may be used as a topping for any hot, moist foods, such as baked potatoes, steamed vegetables, pasta, rice, or hot cereal. The liquefied Mix works particularly well as a base for sauces, as a marinade for basting grilled foods, or brushed over corn on the cob like melted butter. To liquefy Butter Buds® Mix, combine one 1/2-ounce packet (8 level teaspoons) with 1/2 cup (4 ounces) of hot tap water. Stir or shake vigorously to dissolve and then pour to serve or use in recipes. The Spread is terrific on breads, muffins, and pancakes.

What's more, all forms of Butter Buds® may be used as an ingredient in low-fat cooking and baking. Many of the recipes in this cookbook incorporate Butter Buds®, and we've included guidelines below for your own recipe modification. By replacing a portion of the butter, margarine, or oil in a recipe with an equivalent amount of Butter Buds® Sprinkles and Mix, you can enjoy great-tasting, healthier versions of your favorite treats. Refer to the following chart to learn how to substitute Butter Buds® Sprinkles and Mix when baking.

Depending upon the type of baked good, you can usually substitute anywhere from 25 to 100 percent of the fat in a recipe with Butter Buds® Sprinkles and Mix. Refer to the following chart for tips on baking with Butter Buds® Sprinkles and Mix. For instance, cakes usually require more fat for proper texture than do quick breads.

Substitution Chart for Baking

BUTTER OR MARGARINE	BUTTER BUDS® MIX (DRY)	BUTTER BUDS® MIX (LIQUEFIED)	BUTTER BUDS® SPRINKLES
1 tablespoon	1 teaspoon	1 tablespoon	3/4 teaspoon
2 tablespoons	2 teaspoons	2 tablespoons	1-1/2 teaspoons
1/4 cup (1/2 stick)	4 teaspoons (1/2 envelope)	1/4 cup	1 tablespoon
1/2 cup (1 stick)	8 teaspoons (1 envelope)	1/2 cup	2 tablespoons
1 cup (2 sticks)	2 envelopes	1 cup	1/4 cup

Butter Buds® Spread is suitable for low-calorie cooking, baking, and frying. For low-calorie cooking, Butter Buds® Spread may be used in place of regular butter, margarine, or oil. Butter Buds® Spread may also replace the fat in a recipe for baked goods, but due to the high water content of all low-calorie spreads, slight recipe modification may be necessary in some instances to ensure the desired results.

Next time you crave the taste of butter, don't worry about fat and calories. Reach for Butter Buds® instead. Your heart, waistline, and taste buds will agree—Butter Buds® are a winner!

Tips for Baking with Butter Buds®

BAKED ITEMS	AMOUNT OF FAT TO BE REPLACED	RECOMMENDED BUTTER BUDS® FORM
CAKES	1/4 to 1/2	Sprinkles or liquefied Mix
PIECRUSTS	1/2	liquefied Mix
COOKIES*	1/4 to 1/2	Sprinkles or dry Mix
QUICK BREADS	3/4 to all**	Sprinkles or liquefied Mix
MUFFINS	up to 1/2	liquefied Mix

*When removing fat, decrease dry ingredients by 1/4 or dough will be too dry.

**When all fat is replaced, use Butter Buds® liquefied Mix.

If you have a sweet tooth but are trying to maintain or lose weight, Sweet 'N Low® granulated sugar substitute can help you enjoy sweet flavor while limiting your intake of calories. While most Americans are familiar with Sweet 'N Low® as a sweetener for coffee, tea, and other hot and cold beverages, we'll teach you more about Sweet 'N Low®'s versatility as an ingredient.

Sweet 'N Low® is 100 percent heat stable, unlike diet sweeteners that contain aspartame, which breaks down under high temperatures. This heat stability is what makes Sweet 'N Low® perfect for low-calorie cooking, baking, freezing, and preserving. Sweet 'N Low®'s sweetening agent, saccharin, has been successfully used in the sweetening of many commercially available products for many years.

Sweet 'N Low® is sold in boxes of individual serving–size packets, each containing 4 calories and the sweetening power of 2 teaspoons of sugar. There are about 30 calories in 2 teaspoons of sugar. Each pink packet contains 1 gram of carbohydrate in the form of dextrose, a fact that should be taken into consideration by people with diabetes.

Sweet 'N Low® is also available in bulk form, which is convenient for home use in cooking and baking. An 8-ounce box contains the concentrated sweetening equivalent of 5 pounds of sugar and includes a plastic, 1/10-ounce serving–size spoon for easy measuring (2 spoonfuls are equivalent to 1 packet of Sweet 'N Low®). Each half-gram serving of bulk Sweet 'N Low® has the sweetening equivalent of one teaspoon of sugar and contains one half gram of carbohydrate.

A variety of recipes in this cookbook, from drinks and desserts to main courses and side dishes, were significantly trimmed down with Sweet 'N Low®. For convenience, recipes that use 3 or more packets of Sweet 'N Low® also show the corresponding amount of bulk Sweet 'N Low® (1 measured teaspoon or more). Refer to the table below when replacing a portion of a recipe's sugar content with Sweet 'N Low®.

How to Substitute Sweet 'N Low® for Sugar

Granulated sugar	1/4 cup	1/3 cup	1/2 cup	1 cup
Sweet 'N Low® Packets	3 packets	4 packets	6 packets	12 packets
Sweet 'N Low® Bulk	1 teaspoon	1-1/4 teaspoons	2 teaspoons	4 teaspoons

Sweet One®

Sweet One® granulated sugar substitute is one of the newer offerings available for people who are trying to limit their consumption of sugar and sweet treats. Available in the United States since 1988, Sweet One® derives its clean, sugarlike taste from a sweetening agent called acesulfame potassium, or acesulfame-K. You may have seen the brand name for this sweetening agent, Sunette, listed as an ingredient in low-sugar or sugar-free dry beverage mixes, gelatin, and pudding mixes.

Due to its heat stability, Sweet One® is ideal for low-calorie cooking, baking, freezing, and preserving. It has no aftertaste, dissolves quickly in hot and cold beverages, and may be used to replace at least half the sugar in most recipes.

Sweet One®, which is available in many supermarkets and chain drugstores nationwide, is sold in boxes of 50 individual serving–size packets. Each light blue packet, which contains the sweetening equivalent of 2 teaspoons of sugar, contains 4 calories and 1 gram of carbohydrate, a fact that should be taken into consideration by people with diabetes. Sweet One® is also sodium-free and safe for people with phenylketonuria (PKU) under the guidance of a health professional.

Try Sweet One® for yourself, both as a tabletop sweetener and as an ingredient. **If you have a taste preference, please note that Sweet One® may be used interchangeably with Sweet 'N Low® in the recipes in this cookbook.** To modify other recipes to contain less sugar, you may refer to the equivalency chart for Sweet 'N Low®, which is also a proper guideline for cooking and baking with Sweet One®.

How to Substitute Sweet One® for Sugar

Sugar	1/4 cup	1/3 cup	1/2 cup	1 cup
Sweet One®	3 packets	4 packets	6 packets	12 packets

History of Cumberland Packing Corporation

For most people, the familiar sight of pink Sweet 'N Low® packets in restaurants, cafeterias and other food service establishments is as American as hot dogs and apple pie.

While the granulated sugar substitute is available in several countries worldwide, the majority of Sweet 'N Low® is manufactured at Cumberland Packing Corporation's headquarters, located in Brooklyn, N.Y. A family-owned and -run business founded in the 1950s, Cumberland revolutionized the sugar industry with automated packaging of individual serving–size portions of sugar. This convenient, economical concept quickly became very popular among the food service industry.

In the late '50s, anticipating the beginning of the health and dietary reform movement in the United States, Cumberland began to explore options for people who were interested in reducing their sugar intake. As a result, the company developed a granulated sweetener that looked and tasted like sugar but had only a fraction of its calories. Named after the title of a favorite family song, "Sweet and Low," what would become the world's leading sugar substitute had arrived.

By 1963, as business with restaurant and industrial clientele continued to grow, overwhelming consumer demand prompted distribution of Sweet 'N Low® through grocery stores and supermarket and drugstore chains. In 1966, in response to genuine enthusiasm for the product, combined with distressing reports of growing numbers of overweight Americans and excessive public consumption of sugar, Cumberland decided to forgo the regular refined sugar business entirely and became focused solely upon creating and marketing the country's premier line of health and diet products. Cumberland did develop a special turbinado sugar, Sugar In The Raw®, an all-natural raw sugar that is refined from the initial pressing of sugar cane. The sugar crystals aren't stripped of any color or flavoring, giving it a natural taste without any additives.

In keeping close tabs on Americans' growing interest in healthy eating, Cumberland was the first to recognize that high blood pressure levels were prime health concerns for many people. In the mid-'60s, Cumberland began marketing Nu-Salt®, a flavorful substitute product ideal for people who are following a reduced-salt or salt-free diet.

In 1979, years before healthy, low-fat eating became a full-blown trend, Cumberland developed Butter Buds® all-natural butter-flavored granulated Mix, the first butter alternative on the market. Although Butter Buds® Mix derived its delicious flavor from real butter, the product was and still is free of fat and cholesterol, while providing a fraction of the calories.

The easy-to-use Mix, which could be liquefied with hot water, was incredibly versatile as a topping and ingredient, quickly garnering praise from health-conscious consumers. Its popularity lead to the introduction of Butter Buds® Sprinkles in 1987, a version that could be shaken onto hot, moist foods or used in cooking and baking.

In 1988, recognizing that people have different tastes, a Cumberland subsidiary introduced Americans to another low-calorie granulated sugar substitute, Sweet One®. Made with an intense sweetening agent called acesulfame-potassium, Sweet One® dissolves quickly in hot and cold beverages, is safe for people with diabetes, and is heat stable for healthy cooking and baking. Consumers welcomed this new choice as another smart option for cutting calories and maintaining a healthy lifestyle.

Most recently, in 1993, Cumberland expanded its line of low-fat butter alternatives with Butter Buds® Spread, a low-fat spread that contains only 25 calories, less than 3 grams of fat per tablespoon serving and 75 percent less fat and calories than regular butter or margarine. Available in both sticks and tubs for convenient use as a topping or ingredient in low-fat cooking and baking, Butter Buds® Spread offers yet another healthful alternative to consumers who want to lower their intake of dietary fat.

For four decades, Cumberland has been committed to meeting the needs of health-conscious people around the globe, with a complete line of products that are low in fat and calories. From Brooklyn to Belgium to Bermuda . . . next time you pick up a familiar pink Sweet 'N Low® packet, you'll know the whole story!

Morning Starts

While breakfast is the most important meal of the day, breakfast foods can be eaten at any meal. Our muffins, quick breads, and traditional breakfast favorites can be made ahead, frozen individually, and heated in the oven, toaster oven, or microwave for a warm and tasty treat anytime. Or try our not-so-traditional breakfast recipes that are sure to become new favorites.

Cinnamon French Toast

YIELD:
6 slices (6 servings)

**PER SERVING
(1 SLICE):**

90 calories

5 g protein

13 g carbohydrate

2 g fat

<1 g saturated fat

35 mg cholesterol

205 mg sodium

**DIABETIC
EXCHANGE:**

1 starch/bread
exchange

1/2 CUP SKIM MILK

1/4 CUP LIQUEFIED BUTTER BUDS MIX

1 LARGE EGG

3 LARGE EGG WHITES

1 TEASPOON VANILLA EXTRACT

2 PACKETS SWEET 'N LOW

1/2 TEASPOON GROUND CINNAMON, PLUS MORE FOR SPRINKLING

6 SLICES REDUCED-CALORIE BREAD

BUTTERY PANCAKE SYRUP, OPTIONAL (PAGE 31)

COUNTRY MAPLE TOPPING, OPTIONAL (PAGE 32)

In a shallow dish, whisk together the milk, Butter Buds, egg, egg whites, vanilla, Sweet 'N Low, and 1/2 teaspoon cinnamon until well blended. Spray a large nonstick skillet with nonstick cooking spray; heat over medium-low heat. Dip the bread slices, one at a time, into the egg mixture, turning once to coat. Place in a skillet and cook 2 to 3 minutes on each side, or until golden. Sprinkle with additional cinnamon. Transfer to a serving platter. Serve with Buttery Pancake Syrup or Country Maple Topping, if desired.

Traditional Pancakes

1/2 CUP ALL-PURPOSE FLOUR

1/2 CUP WHOLE WHEAT FLOUR

2 TABLESPOONS SUGAR

1 TEASPOON BAKING POWDER

1/2 TEASPOON BAKING SODA

1 CUP BUTTERMILK

1/4 CUP LIQUEFIED BUTTER BUDS MIX

1 LARGE EGG

BUTTERY PANCAKE SYRUP, OPTIONAL (PAGE 31)

COUNTRY MAPLE TOPPING, OPTIONAL (PAGE 32)

Spray a large nonstick skillet with nonstick cooking spray; heat over medium-low heat. In a medium bowl, combine the flours, sugar, baking powder, and baking soda. In another bowl, combine the buttermilk, Butter Buds, and egg; add to dry ingredients, stirring just until blended. Pour 1/4 cup batter into prepared skillet. Heat 3 to 4 minutes, or until golden. Repeat, using up batter. Remove to a serving plate and keep warm. Serve with Buttery Pancake Syrup or Country Maple Topping, if desired.

YIELD:
12 pancakes
(6 servings)

**PER SERVING
(2 PANCAKES):**

125 calories

5 g protein

24 g carbohydrate

1 g fat

1 g saturated fat

35 mg cholesterol

170 mg sodium

**DIABETIC
EXCHANGES:**

1-1/2 starch/bread
exchanges

YIELD:
12 pancakes
(6 servings)

**PER SERVING
(2 PANCAKES):**

130 calories

4 g protein

26 g carbohydrate

1 g fat

<1 g saturated fat

35 mg cholesterol

160 mg sodium

**DIABETIC
EXCHANGES:**

2 starch/bread
exchanges

YIELD:
12 pancakes
(6 servings)

**PER SERVING
(2 PANCAKES):**

145 calories

5 g protein

28 g carbohydrate

2 g fat

1 g saturated fat

35 mg cholesterol

175 mg sodium

**DIABETIC
EXCHANGES:**

2 starch/bread
exchanges

Apple-Cinnamon Pancakes

Add *1 teaspoon ground cinnamon* to dry ingredients. Reduce the buttermilk to 3/4 cup; stir *1/2 cup unsweetened applesauce* into liquid ingredients. Proceed as directed.

Blueberry Cornmeal Pancakes

Omit the whole wheat flour; add *1/2 cup yellow cornmeal* to dry ingredients. Let stand 5 minutes to thicken slightly and proceed as directed except: As the pancakes are cooking, press *1 cup unsweetened fresh or frozen blueberries* into the pancakes (6 to 8 blueberries per pancake); flip and continue cooking until golden.

TIP: In recipes such as pancakes and French toast, leaving one egg yolk in the batter helps keep it tender. Too many egg whites produce a tough product.

Buttery Pancake Syrup

1 PACKET BUTTER BUDS MIX, DRY

3/4 CUP REDUCED-CALORIE MAPLE FLAVORED SYRUP

In a small saucepan, beat the Butter Buds into the syrup until well blended (Butter Buds will not be dissolved). Over low heat, simmer until dissolved, stirring frequently. Serve.

YIELD:
3/4 cup
(12 servings)

**PER SERVING
(1 TABLESPOON):**

30 calories

0 g protein

8 g carbohydrate

0 g fat

0 g saturated fat

0 mg cholesterol

75 mg sodium

**DIABETIC
EXCHANGE:**

1/2 fruit exchange

Country Maple Topping

YIELD:
3/4 cup
(12 servings)

PER SERVING
(1 TABLESPOON):

10 calories

0 g protein

3 g carbohydrate

0 g fat

0 g saturated fat

0 mg cholesterol

50 mg sodium

DIABETIC
EXCHANGE:

Free exchange

3/4 CUP WATER

1 PACKET BUTTER BUDS MIX, DRY

1 TABLESPOON SUGAR

2 PACKETS SWEET 'N LOW

1 TEASPOON CORNSTARCH

1/2 TEASPOON MAPLE FLAVORING

In a small saucepan, combine all the ingredients except the maple flavoring; cook over medium heat, stirring constantly, until the mixture comes to a boil and thickens. Stir in the maple flavoring and serve.

MICROWAVE DIRECTIONS: In a 1-cup microwavable measure, combine all the ingredients except the maple flavoring. Cook, uncovered, on 100% power 2 to 3 minutes, or until bubbly. Stir; cook an additional 30 seconds, or until thickened. Stir until smooth and serve.

Easy Sticky Buns

1 PACKET BUTTER BUDS MIX, DRY

1/4 CUP HOT WATER

3 TABLESPOONS PACKED LIGHT BROWN SUGAR

1-1/2 TEASPOONS GROUND CINNAMON

1-1/2 TABLESPOONS CHOPPED WALNUTS

1 PACKAGE (7.5 OUNCES) REFRIGERATED BISCUITS

Preheat the oven to 375°F. Spray an 8-inch round baking pan with nonstick cooking spray.

In a small bowl, combine the Butter Buds, water, brown sugar, and cinnamon; pour into a prepared pan. Sprinkle with nuts. Arrange the biscuits in a single layer on top of the nuts.

Bake 15 to 20 minutes, or until well browned. Immediately invert onto a serving plate.

YIELD:
10 buns
(10 servings)

**PER SERVING
(1 BUN):**

80 calories

1 g protein

16 g carbohydrate

2 g fat

<1 g saturated fat

0 mg cholesterol

240 mg sodium

**DIABETIC
EXCHANGE:**

1 starch/bread
exchange

YIELD:
12 muffins
(12 servings)

**PER SERVING
(1 MUFFIN):**

140 calories

4 g protein

30 g carbohydrate

1 g fat

<1 g saturated fat

20 mg cholesterol

65 mg sodium

**DIABETIC
EXCHANGES:**

1-1/2 starch/bread
exchanges

1 fruit exchange

Blueberry Muffins

2-1/4 CUPS ALL-PURPOSE FLOUR, DIVIDED

1/2 CUP SUGAR

1 TABLESPOON BAKING POWDER

1/8 TEASPOON SALT

3/4 CUP 1% FAT MILK

1/4 CUP LIQUEFIED BUTTER BUDS MIX

1 LARGE EGG

1-1/2 CUPS FRESH OR FROZEN (THAWED) UNSWEETENED BLUEBERRIES

Preheat the oven to 400°F. Spray a 12-cup muffin pan with nonstick cooking spray or line with paper muffin cups.

In a large bowl, combine 2 cups flour, sugar, baking powder, and salt. Combine the milk, Butter Buds, and egg; stir into the dry ingredients until moistened. Rinse and drain the blueberries; toss with the remaining 1/4 cup flour. Gently fold into the batter. Spoon equal amounts of batter into the prepared muffin cups.

Bake 20 to 25 minutes, or until golden brown and a toothpick inserted in the center comes out clean. Remove from the pan and cool on a wire rack.

Orange-Vanilla Muffins

2 CUPS SIFTED ALL-PURPOSE FLOUR

2 TABLESPOONS SUGAR

6 PACKETS (OR 2 TEASPOONS BULK) SWEET 'N LOW

2-1/2 TEASPOONS BAKING POWDER

1/2 TEASPOON BAKING SODA

1 CUP BUTTERMILK

1/4 CUP REDUCED-CALORIE TUB MARGARINE, MELTED

1/4 CUP ORANGE JUICE

1 LARGE EGG

2 TEASPOONS FINELY GRATED ORANGE RIND

1 TEASPOON VANILLA EXTRACT

Preheat the oven to 400°F. Spray a 12-cup muffin pan with nonstick cooking spray or line with paper muffin cups.

In a large bowl, sift the dry ingredients. In another bowl, combine the buttermilk, margarine, orange juice, egg, orange rind, and vanilla. Make a well in the center of the dry ingredients. Pour in the liquid ingredients; stir until moistened. Spoon equal amounts of batter into the prepared muffin cups.

Bake 15 to 18 minutes, or until golden brown and a toothpick inserted in the center comes out clean. Cool in the pan on a wire rack 5 minutes. Remove from the pan; serve warm or cold.

TIP: Buttermilk helps produce a slightly more tender product in low-fat baked goods.

YIELD:
12 muffins
(12 servings)

**PER SERVING
(1 MUFFIN):**

120 calories

3 g protein

20 g carbohydrate

3 g fat

1 g saturated fat

20 mg cholesterol

85 mg sodium

**DIABETIC
EXCHANGES:**

1 starch/bread
exchange

1/2 fat exchange

YIELD:
12 muffins
(12 servings)

**PER SERVING
(1 MUFFIN):**

125 calories

3 g protein

20 g carbohydrate

3 g fat,

1 g saturated fat

20 mg cholesterol

85 mg sodium

**DIABETIC
EXCHANGES:**

1 starch/bread
exchange

1/2 fat exchange

Lemon Poppy Seed Muffins

Replace the orange juice with *2 tablespoons lemon juice*; replace the orange rind with *lemon rind*. Proceed as directed; stir *1 tablespoon poppy seeds* into the prepared batter. Bake as directed.

Honey Raisin Bran Muffins

3/4 CUP HOT WATER

1 PACKET BUTTER BUDS MIX, DRY

1 CUP UNPROCESSED WHEAT BRAN, DIVIDED

1/2 CUP ALL-PURPOSE FLOUR

1/2 CUP WHOLE WHEAT FLOUR

1-1/2 TEASPOONS BAKING SODA

1/8 TEASPOON SALT

3/4 CUP BUTTERMILK

1/3 CUP HONEY

1 LARGE EGG

1/2 CUP RAISINS

Preheat the oven to 400°F. Spray a 12-cup muffin pan with nonstick cooking spray or line with paper muffin cups.

In a large bowl, combine the water and Butter Buds until dissolved; stir in 1/2 cup bran and set aside. In another bowl, combine the remaining 1/2 cup bran, the flours, baking soda, and salt. Stir together the buttermilk, honey, and egg. Add the liquid and dry ingredients to the moistened bran mixture; stir until blended. Stir in the raisins. Spoon equal amounts of batter into the prepared muffin cups.

Bake 20 minutes, or until golden brown and a toothpick in the center comes out clean. Remove from the pan and cool slightly on a wire rack. Serve warm or cold.

TIP: Muffin batter may be baked in minimuffin tins for approximately 10 to 12 minutes to yield approximately 36 to 42 muffins.

YIELD:
12 muffins
(12 servings)

**PER SERVING
(1 MUFFIN):**

105 calories

3 g protein

23 g carbohydrate

1 g fat

<1 g saturated fat

20 mg cholesterol

175 mg sodium

**DIABETIC
EXCHANGES:**

1 starch/bread exchange

1/2 fruit exchange

Applesauce Nut Bread

YIELD:
1 loaf or sixteen
1/2-inch slices
(16 servings)

**PER SERVING
(1 SLICE):**

105 calories

2 g protein

17 g carbohydrate

3 g fat

<1 g saturated fat

15 mg cholesterol

65 mg sodium

**DIABETIC
EXCHANGES:**

1/2 starch/bread
exchange

1/2 fruit exchange

1/2 fat exchange

1 CUP SIFTED ALL-PURPOSE FLOUR

3/4 CUP WHOLE WHEAT FLOUR

1/3 CUP SUGAR

6 PACKETS (OR 2 TEASPOONS BULK) SWEET 'N LOW

1 TABLESPOON BAKING POWDER

1/2 TEASPOON EACH: BAKING SODA, GROUND CINNAMON, AND
GROUND NUTMEG

1/8 TEASPOON SALT

1/4 CUP CHOPPED WALNUTS

1 CUP UNSWEETENED APPLESAUCE

1/4 CUP REDUCED-CALORIE TUB MARGARINE, MELTED

1 LARGE EGG

Preheat the oven to 350°F. Spray an 8 × 5 × 2-1/2-inch loaf pan with non-stick cooking spray.

In a large bowl, sift the dry ingredients; stir in the nuts. Combine the applesauce, margarine, and egg; add to the dry ingredients and stir until blended. Pour batter into the prepared pan.

Bake 40 minutes, or until a toothpick inserted in the center comes out clean. Cool in the pan on a wire rack 10 minutes. Remove from the pan and cool completely before slicing.

TIP: Fruits and vegetables—such as apples, bananas, carrots, and zucchini—used in making breads and muffins release their moisture while baking and keep the baked goods tender.

Cranberry-Walnut Bread

2-1/4 CUPS SIFTED ALL-PURPOSE FLOUR

3/4 CUP SUGAR

1 TABLESPOON BAKING POWDER

1/2 TEASPOON BAKING SODA

1/8 TEASPOON SALT

1/2 CUP 1% FAT MILK *OR* BUTTERMILK

1 PACKET BUTTER BUDS MIX, LIQUEFIED

1 LARGE EGG

1 TEASPOON GRATED ORANGE RIND

1 CUP CHOPPED FRESH OR FROZEN (UNTHAWED) CRANBERRIES

1/4 CUP CHOPPED WALNUTS

Preheat the oven to 350°F. Spray a 9 × 5-inch loaf pan with nonstick cooking spray.

In a large bowl, sift the dry ingredients. Combine the milk, Butter Buds, egg, and orange rind; stir into the dry ingredients until moistened. Add the cranberries and walnuts. Spoon the batter into a prepared pan.

Bake 45 minutes, or until toothpick inserted in the center comes out clean. Cool in the pan on a wire rack 10 minutes. Remove from the pan and cool completely before slicing.

TIP: For quick serving, wrap individual slices of bread in plastic wrap and freeze. Muffins may be frozen, individually covered with wax paper, on a cookie sheet; when firm, place in a plastic bag. To serve, heat muffins or slices of bread in a microwave at high power for 30 to 60 seconds or a 400°F oven for 10 minutes.

YIELD:
1 loaf or eighteen
1/2-inch slices
(18 servings)

**PER SERVING
(1 SLICE):**

110 calories

3 g protein

22 g carbohydrate

1 g fat

<1 g saturated fat

10 mg cholesterol

80 mg sodium

**DIABETIC
EXCHANGES:**

1 starch/bread
exchange

1/2 fruit exchange

Fresh Fruit Kabobs

YIELD:
12 skewers
(6 servings)

**PER SERVING
(2 SKEWERS):**

25 calories

<1 g protein

7 g carbohydrate

<1 g fat

<1 g saturated fat

0 mg cholesterol

5 mg sodium

**DIABETIC
EXCHANGE:**

1/2 fruit exchange

**3 CUPS ASSORTED FRESH FRUIT SLICES OR WEDGES,
SUCH AS APPLES, BANANAS, ORANGES, PLUMS, PINEAPPLE,
AND WHOLE STRAWBERRIES**

**2 TABLESPOONS LEMON JUICE MIXED WITH
1 QUART COLD WATER**

12 WOODEN SKEWERS

HONEY YOGURT CREAM, OPTIONAL (PAGE 137)

Drop fruit slices in lemon water to prevent discoloration. Thread equal amounts of fruit on the skewers. Serve with Honey Yogurt Cream, if desired.

TIP: Fresh fruit is an excellent source of dietary fiber and many nutrients. It is also a healthy choice to satisfy your sweet tooth.

Spanish Potato Omelet

3 CUPS DICED PEELED POTATOES (1-1/4 POUNDS UNPEELED)

1-1/2 CUPS CHOPPED ONION (2 MEDIUM)

1 PACKET BUTTER BUDS MIX, LIQUEFIED, DIVIDED

1 CUP LIQUID EGG SUBSTITUTE

2 LARGE EGGS

2 TEASPOONS SALT-FREE GARLIC-AND-HERB SEASONING BLEND

2 TABLESPOONS MINCED FRESH PARSLEY

1/8 TEASPOON EACH: SALT AND PEPPER

RED PEPPER PUREE, OPTIONAL (PAGE 55)

Heat the oven to broil.

Cook the potatoes in unsalted water to cover 15 to 20 minutes, or until tender. Drain; pat dry with paper towel.

Meanwhile, spray a 10-inch nonstick skillet with nonstick cooking spray. Over medium heat, cook the onion in 1/4 cup Butter Buds until tender; stir in the potatoes.

In a small bowl, combine the remaining Butter Buds with the remaining ingredients, except the Red Pepper Puree. Pour into the skillet. Cook, covered, over low heat 5 minutes, or until almost set. Cover the skillet handle with aluminum foil. With the oven door partially open, broil the omelet 3 to 4 inches from the heat source 1 minute, or until set and lightly browned. Cut into wedges; serve from the skillet. Serve with Red Pepper Puree, if desired.

TIP: When using fresh herbs, use 3 times the amount suggested for dried herbs.

YIELD:
6 servings

PER SERVING:

180 calories

10 g protein

28 g carbohydrate

3 g fat

1 g saturated fat

70 mg cholesterol

245 mg sodium

DIABETIC EXCHANGES:

2 starch/bread exchanges

1 lean meat exchange

℔℔

Zucchini Frittata

YIELD:
8 servings

**PER SERVING
(1 WEDGE):**

65 calories

5 g protein

6 g carbohydrate

2 g fat

1 g saturated fat

55 mg cholesterol

155 mg sodium

**DIABETIC
EXCHANGES:**

1 vegetable
exchange

1/2 lean meat
exchange

1 MEDIUM ZUCCHINI, JULIENNE CUT (ABOUT 2 CUPS)

1 MEDIUM RED OR YELLOW BELL PEPPER, JULIENNE CUT
(ABOUT 1 CUP)

1/2 MEDIUM LEEK, JULIENNE CUT (ABOUT 3/4 CUP)

1 TEASPOON THYME LEAVES, CRUSHED

1 PACKET BUTTER BUDS MIX, LIQUEFIED, DIVIDED

3/4 CUP LIQUID EGG SUBSTITUTE

2 LARGE EGGS

3 TABLESPOONS FAT-FREE PARMESAN CHEESE TOPPING, DIVIDED

1/8 TEASPOON EACH: GARLIC POWDER AND PEPPER

Spray a large nonstick skillet with nonstick cooking spray; heat over medium-high heat. Add the vegetables, thyme, and 1/4 cup Butter Buds; cook, covered, 2 minutes. Uncover; reduce the heat to medium-low.

In a small bowl, combine the remaining 1/4 cup Butter Buds, egg substitute, eggs, 2 tablespoons cheese topping, garlic, and pepper. Pour over the vegetables, spreading the vegetables evenly in skillet. Cook, covered, 5 minutes, or until almost set.

Meanwhile, heat the oven to broil. Cover the skillet handle with aluminum foil. Sprinkle the frittata with the remaining 1 tablespoon cheese topping. With the oven door partially open, broil the frittata 3 to 4 inches from the heat source for 1 minute, or until set and lightly browned. Cut into 8 wedges; serve from the skillet.

Light Bites

For a sensational brunch, a quick snack, a special lunch, or a late-night meal, our Light Bites will tantalize your taste buds. Selections such as our Spicy Shrimp, Pepper Medley Pizza, and Pita Crisps with Crabmeat Dip will satisfy even the most discriminating of connoisseurs.

YIELD:
12 potato skins
(12 servings)

**PER SERVING
(1 SKIN):**

70 calories

1 g protein

14 g carbohydrate

1 g fat

<1 g saturated fat

0 mg cholesterol

20 mg sodium

**DIABETIC
EXCHANGE:**

1 starch/bread
exchange

YIELD:
24 pieces
(24 servings)

**PER SERVING
(1 STRIP):**

35 calories

1 g protein

7 g carbohydrate

1 g fat

0 g saturated fat

0 mg cholesterol

10 mg sodium

**DIABETIC
EXCHANGE:**

1/2 starch/bread
exchange

Baked Potato Skins

6 MEDIUM UNCOOKED IDAHO POTATOES (ABOUT 1-3/4 POUNDS)

2 TABLESPOONS LIQUEFIED BUTTER BUDS MIX

1 TABLESPOON OLIVE OIL

**1 TEASPOON SALT-FREE GARLIC-AND-HERB SEASONING BLEND
(OR YOUR FAVORITE SALT-FREE BLEND)**

Preheat the oven to 400°F. Scrub the potatoes under cold water; pat dry. Prick in several places with a fork. Bake for 1 hour. Remove from the oven and cool slightly.

In a small bowl, stir together the Butter Buds, oil, and seasoning. Cut the potatoes in half lengthwise; scoop out the pulp, leaving a 1/4-inch-thick shell. Brush the shells with the Butter Buds mixture. Place on a cookie sheet and bake 15 minutes, or until lightly crisped.

SERVING SUGGESTION: Leftover potato pulp can be mashed with fresh steamed broccoli or cauliflower and skim milk and seasoned with Butter Buds, salt, and pepper for a light side dish.

Leftover potato pulp can be whipped (mashed) with skim milk, Butter Buds, salt, and pepper and added back to baked potato skins.

TIP: The leftover potato pulp is great for thickening soups, stews, and sauces without additional fat.

TIP: Potatoes with their skins are high in dietary fiber, vitamin C, and potassium.

Potato Skin Strips

After scooping out the pulp, cut each shell in half again lengthwise. Proceed as directed. Bake 12 to 15 minutes, or until lightly crisped.

Pizza Potato Skins

12 BAKED POTATO SKINS (PAGE 44)

1 CUP BASIC MARINARA SAUCE (PAGE 94)

3/4 CUP (3 OUNCES) SHREDDED REDUCED-FAT
MOZZARELLA CHEESE

DRIED OREGANO, CRUMBLED

1 OUNCE SLICED PEPPERONI, CHOPPED OR SLIVERED, OPTIONAL

1 TABLESPOON FAT-FREE GRATED PARMESAN ITALIAN TOPPING

Preheat the oven to 400°F. Place the potato skins on a cookie sheet. Spoon about 1 tablespoon Basic Marinara Sauce into each shell. Sprinkle the mozzarella cheese evenly into the shells; sprinkle with oregano. Top with pepperoni, if desired; sprinkle with the Parmesan topping. Bake 12 to 15 minutes, or until the cheese is melted.

YIELD:
12 potato skins
(12 servings)

**PER SERVING
(1 SKIN):**

90 calories

3 g protein

15 g carbohydrate

2 g fat

1 g saturated fat

5 mg cholesterol

95 mg sodium

**DIABETIC
EXCHANGE:**

1 starch/bread
exchange

Cheddar Potato Skins

YIELD:
12 potato skins
(12 servings)

**PER SERVING
(1 SKIN):**

100 calories

4 g protein

15 g carbohydrate

2 g fat

1 g saturated fat

5 mg cholesterol

85 mg sodium

**DIABETIC
EXCHANGE:**

1 starch/bread
exchange

12 BAKED POTATO SKINS (PAGE 44)

1/2 CUP NONFAT SOUR CREAM

1/4 CUP THINLY SLICED SCALLIONS

2 TABLESPOONS BACON-FLAVOR CHIPS, OPTIONAL

3/4 CUP (3 OUNCES) SHREDDED REDUCED-FAT CHEDDAR CHEESE

Preheat the oven to 400°F. Place the potato skin shells on a cookie sheet. Spoon about 2 teaspoons sour cream into each shell, spreading with the back of the spoon. Sprinkle the scallions evenly into the shells. Sprinkle evenly with bacon chips, if desired. Top with grated cheese. Bake 12 to 15 minutes, or until the cheese is melted.

Chicken Fingers

1-1/2 CUPS CORNFLAKES

1 PACKET BUTTER BUDS MIX, DRY (OR 2 TABLESPOONS BUTTER BUDS SPRINKLES), DIVIDED

1 TABLESPOON SALT-FREE GARLIC-AND-HERB SEASONING BLEND

1/8 TEASPOON EACH: DRY MUSTARD, SALT, AND PEPPER

1/4 CUP HOT WATER

1 LARGE EGG WHITE

1 POUND SKINLESS, BONELESS CHICKEN BREASTS, CUT INTO STRIPS

HONEY-MUSTARD DIP, OPTIONAL (PAGE 95)

HORSERADISH DIP, OPTIONAL (PAGE 96)

BASIC MARINARA SAUCE, OPTIONAL (PAGE 94)

YIELD:
20 pieces
(10 servings)

**PER SERVING
(2 PIECES):**

90 calories

10 g protein

6 g carbohydrate

2 g fat

<1 g saturated fat

30 mg cholesterol

130 mg sodium

**DIABETIC
EXCHANGES:**

1/2 starch/bread
exchange

1 lean meat
exchange

In a food processor or blender, combine the cornflakes, 1/2 packet (4 teaspoons) Butter Buds Mix (or 1 tablespoon Butter Buds Sprinkles), and seasonings. Process until the cornflakes are fine crumbs. Pour the crumbs into a shallow dish. Combine the remaining 4 teaspoons Butter Buds Mix (or 1 tablespoon Butter Buds Sprinkles) with hot water to dissolve. Whisk in the egg white with a fork until well blended and pour into another shallow dish.

Heat the oven to 400°F. Spray a cookie sheet with nonstick cooking spray. Dip the chicken strips into the egg white mixture, then into the crumb mixture. Place on the prepared cookie sheet.

Bake 12 to 15 minutes, turning once, until golden and cooked through. Serve with Honey-Mustard Dip, Horseradish Dip, or Basic Marinara Sauce, if desired.

TIP: Many stores carry chicken "tenders" (the tenderloin of the chicken breast)—the perfect size for chicken fingers. To easily remove the little white tendon: Place the chicken tender on a cutting board, tendon-side down. With one hand, hold the tendon; with a small sharp knife in the other hand, gently push the flesh away from the tendon until the tendon is removed; discard.

YIELD:
24 shrimp
(12 servings)

**PER SERVING
(2 SHRIMP):**
45 calories
7 g protein
1 g carbohydrate
1 g fat
<1 g saturated fat
65 mg cholesterol
185 mg sodium

**DIABETIC
EXCHANGE:**
1 lean meat
exchange

YIELD:
6 servings

**PER SERVING
(4 SHRIMP WITH
VEGETABLES):**
170 calories
20 g protein
11 g carbohydrate
5 g fat
1 g saturated fat
195 mg cholesterol
553 mg sodium

**DIABETIC
EXCHANGES:**
2 vegetable
exchanges
2 lean meat
exchanges

Spicy Shrimp

1 PACKET BUTTER BUDS MIX, LIQUEFIED

2 TABLESPOONS MINCED FRESH PARSLEY

1-1/2 TEASPOONS CAJUN SEASONING

1 TABLESPOON OLIVE OIL

1 LARGE GARLIC CLOVE, MINCED

1 POUND JUMBO SHRIMP, PEELED AND DEVEINED
(ABOUT 24 SHRIMP)

Preheat the oven to 400°F.

In a medium bowl, combine all the ingredients except the shrimp. Add the shrimp and toss to coat. Cover and refrigerate 1 hour. Transfer the shrimp and the marinade to a baking dish large enough to hold the shrimp in a single layer. Bake 10 minutes, or until cooked through. Do not overcook. Serve hot or at room temperature with toothpicks.

Shrimp-Vegetable Medley

To serve as a main dish, after refrigeration stir *4 cups assorted raw vegetables (such as small whole mushrooms, bell peppers, and zucchini chunks)* into shrimp. Bake as directed.

Pita Crisps

3 WHOLE WHEAT MINI PITA BREADS
2 TABLESPOONS LIQUEFIED BUTTER BUDS MIX
1 TABLESPOON OLIVE OIL
1 TEASPOON SALT-FREE GARLIC-AND-HERB SEASONING BLEND
(OR YOUR FAVORITE SALT-FREE BLEND)

Preheat the oven to 400°F. Cut mini pita breads completely around the edges to make 6 circles. In a small bowl, stir together the Butter Buds, oil, and seasoning. Brush the pitas with the Butter Buds mixture. Cut each circle into quarters. Bake 7 to 10 minutes, or until golden.

TIP: Need a quick, low-calorie, low-fat snack idea? Top air-popped popcorn with Butter Buds Sprinkles!

YIELD:
24 pieces
(6 servings)

**PER SERVING
(4 PIECES):**

55 calories

2 g protein

7 g carbohydrate

2 g fat

<1 g saturated fat

0 mg cholesterol

100 mg sodium

**DIABETIC
EXCHANGE:**

1/2 starch/bread
exchange

Crabmeat Dip

YIELD:
1-3/4 cups
(14 servings)

**PER SERVING
(2
TABLESPOONS):**

30 calories

5 g protein

2 g carbohydrate

<1 g fat

<1 g saturated fat

10 mg cholesterol

155 mg sodium

**DIABETIC
EXCHANGE:**

1/2 lean meat
exchange

1 CONTAINER (8 OUNCES) NONFAT PASTEURIZED PROCESS
CREAM CHEESE PRODUCT, SOFTENED

1/4 CUP NONFAT SOUR CREAM

1/3 CUP FINELY CHOPPED ONION

1 TABLESPOON PREPARED HORSERADISH

1-1/2 TEASPOONS BUTTER BUDS SPRINKLES

FRESHLY GROUND BLACK PEPPER, TO TASTE

1 CAN (6-1/2 OUNCES) CRABMEAT, DRAINED, RINSED, AND FLAKED

1 TABLESPOON FRESH LEMON JUICE

1 PACKET SWEET 'N LOW

PITA CRISPS (PAGE 49)

BAKED POTATO SKINS (PAGE 44)

ASSORTED RAW VEGETABLES

In a food processor, process the cream cheese until smooth. Transfer to a medium bowl and stir in the sour cream until well blended, then the onion, horseradish, Butter Buds, and pepper to taste. Stir in the crabmeat, lemon juice, and Sweet 'N Low. Chill 30 minutes for the flavors to blend. Serve with Pita Crisps, Baked Potato Skins, or raw vegetables.

NOTE: For Hot Crabmeat Dip, bake, covered, in a preheated 400°F oven 15 minutes, or until heated through. Stir before serving. Great as a dip or filling for Baked Potato Skins.

Garden Fresh Salsa

1-1/2 POUNDS TOMATOES, PEELED

1 MEDIUM ONION, CHOPPED

1 LARGE BELL PEPPER, CHOPPED

1/3 CUP DISTILLED WHITE VINEGAR

1/4 CUP CHOPPED FRESH CILANTRO

1 GARLIC CLOVE, MINCED

1/2 TEASPOON CHILI POWDER

1/4 TEASPOON CUMIN

1/4 TEASPOON SALT

1 PACKET SWEET 'N LOW

1/8 TEASPOON BLACK PEPPER

1/8 TEASPOON RED PEPPER FLAKES, OPTIONAL

Cut the tomatoes in half crosswise; gently squeeze into a colander set over a bowl to remove the seeds, and reserve the juice. Discard the seeds. Chop the tomatoes and place in a bowl with the juice. Stir in the remaining ingredients. Cover and refrigerate several hours before serving.

NOTE: Salsa can be cooked over medium heat about 30 minutes, or until thick, if desired, to make 2-1/4 cups.

TIP: Salsas are a low-fat alternative to traditional sour cream dips. Try dipping into salsa with low-fat Pita Crisps (page 49) or Baked Potato Skins (page 44).

YIELD:
4 cups (16 servings)

PER SERVING (1/4 CUP):

15 calories

1 g protein

3 g carbohydrate

<1 g fat

<1 g saturated fat

0 mg cholesterol

5 mg sodium

DIABETIC EXCHANGE:

Free exchange

Taco Dip

**4 OUNCES NONFAT PASTEURIZED PROCESS CREAM CHEESE
PRODUCT, SOFTENED**

1/2 CUP NONFAT SOUR CREAM

1/2 CUP YOGURT CHEESE (PAGE 53)

3/4 TEASPOON BUTTER BUDS SPRINKLES

FEW DROPS HOT RED PEPPER SAUCE

1-1/4 CUPS COOKED GARDEN FRESH SALSA (PAGE 51)

1 MEDIUM GREEN BELL PEPPER, DICED (3/4 CUP)

1 MEDIUM TOMATO, DICED (3/4 CUP)

2 CUPS SHREDDED LETTUCE

**1/2 CUP (2 OUNCES) SHREDDED REDUCED-FAT
SHARP CHEDDAR CHEESE**

PITA CRISPS, OPTIONAL (PAGE 49)

In a food processor, process the cream cheese until smooth; scrape into a bowl. Stir in the sour cream, yogurt cheese, Butter Buds, and hot red pepper sauce, followed by the Garden Fresh Salsa. Spread the mixture in the bottom of a large shallow dish. The mixture may be refrigerated at this point for several hours or overnight, if desired. Sprinkle the bell pepper and tomato over the salsa mixture. Top with shredded lettuce and cheese. Cover and refrigerate until ready to serve. Serve with Pita Crisps, if desired.

Yogurt Cheese

Place *1 pint plain nonfat yogurt* in a colander lined with cheesecloth or a dampened paper coffee filter and place over a deep bowl. Cover and refrigerate 6 to 8 hours, or until thick. Discard the liquid. The cheese can be used as an ingredient in recipes or as a topping in place of sour cream.

NOTE: Yogurt Cheese is used as an ingredient in recipes throughout this book.

YIELD:
1 cup (4 servings)

**PER SERVING
(1/4 CUP):**

60 calories

6 g protein

9 g carbohydrate

0 g fat

0 g saturated fat

<1 mg cholesterol

80 mg sodium

**DIABETIC
EXCHANGE:**

1/2 nonfat milk
exchange

Chicken Fajitas

YIELD:
6 fajitas (6 servings)

PER SERVING
(1 FAJITA):

190 calories

16 g protein

19 g carbohydrate

6 g fat

2 g saturated fat

35 mg cholesterol

220 mg sodium

DIABETIC
EXCHANGES:

1 starch/bread
exchange

1-1/2 lean meat
exchanges

3/4 CUP REDUCED-SODIUM CHICKEN BROTH

2 TABLESPOONS RED WINE VINEGAR

1 TABLESPOON BUTTER BUDS SPRINKLES

1/2 TEASPOON CHILI POWDER, OR TO TASTE

1/2 TEASPOON DRIED OREGANO, CRUMBLED

1/4 TEASPOON GROUND CUMIN

8 OUNCES COOKED CHICKEN BREAST, CUT INTO STRIPS

1 LARGE RED BELL PEPPER, CUT INTO THIN STRIPS

6 FLOUR TORTILLAS

1/4 CUP (1 OUNCE) SHREDDED REDUCED-FAT
SHARP CHEDDAR OR MOZZARELLA CHEESE

RED PEPPER PUREE, OPTIONAL (PAGE 55)

In a medium skillet, combine the broth, vinegar, Butter Buds, chili powder, oregano, and cumin. Simmer 10 minutes. Add the chicken and red pepper; heat, covered, 5 to 10 minutes, or until most of the liquid has been absorbed and the red pepper is tender. Remove from the heat.

Preheat the oven to 375°F.

Wrap the tortillas in microwavable plastic wrap; place in a microwave and cook at 100% power 30 seconds, or until softened (or heat tortillas, one at a time, in a warm, dry skillet). Spread out the tortillas on a flat surface. Spoon equal amounts of the chicken mixture on each tortilla; sprinkle with equal amounts of cheese. Roll up the tortillas and place seam-side down in a single layer in a baking pan; bake until heated through. Serve with Red Pepper Puree, if desired.

TIP: When preparing Chicken Fajitas, use 2 leftover Rosemary Roasted Chicken Breasts (page 98), if desired, or brown two 4-ounce chicken cutlets in a small nonstick skillet. Add the marinade and heat, covered, until cooked through.

Red Pepper Puree

2 LARGE RED BELL PEPPERS

1/4 CUP CHOPPED ONION

1/4 CUP REDUCED-SODIUM CHICKEN BROTH

1 LARGE GARLIC CLOVE, MINCED

1-1/2 TEASPOONS BUTTER BUDS SPRINKLES

Roast the peppers over an open flame or under a broiler until the skin blisters on all sides. Place in a paper bag at least 10 minutes, or until cool enough to handle. Peel off the skin; cut the peppers into chunks. Place in a saucepan with the remaining ingredients. Cook over high heat until the mixture comes to a boil. Reduce the heat to low; cover and cook 10 minutes, or until tender. In a food processor or blender, puree the mixture. Pour into a serving container. Serve warm or at room temperature.

YIELD:
1-1/4 cups
(5 servings)

**PER SERVING
(1/4 CUP):**

15 calories

1 g protein

4 g carbohydrate

<1 g fat

0 g saturated fat

0 mg cholesterol

25 mg sodium

**DIABETIC
EXCHANGE:**

Free exchange

YIELD:
1 nine-inch pie
(6 servings)

**PER SERVING
(1 WEDGE):**

155 calories

14 g protein

15 g carbohydrates

6 g fat

2 g saturated fat

45 mg cholesterol

350 mg sodium

**DIABETIC
EXCHANGES:**

1/2 starch/bread
exchange

1 vegetable
exchange

1-1/2 lean meat
exchanges

Crusty Cheddar-Broccoli Pie

1/3 CUP CHOPPED ONION
1 PACKET BUTTER BUDS MIX, MIXED WITH 1/4 CUP HOT WATER
1 PACKAGE (10 OUNCES) FROZEN CHOPPED BROCCOLI
3/4 CUP (3 OUNCES) SHREDDED REDUCED-FAT
MILD CHEDDAR CHEESE, DIVIDED
4 SHEETS PHYLLO DOUGH
1 CUP LIQUID EGG SUBSTITUTE
1 LARGE EGG
1 TEASPOON SALT-FREE LEMON-AND-PEPPER SPICE BLEND
1/4 TEASPOON GROUND NUTMEG
1/8 TEASPOON GARLIC POWDER

Preheat the oven to 375°F.

In a medium skillet over medium heat, cook the onion in the Butter Buds mixture until softened; remove from the heat. Stir in the broccoli and 1/2 cup cheese; set aside.

Spray a 9-inch pie pan with nonstick cooking spray. Place the phyllo on a flat surface; keep covered with a damp cloth or plastic wrap to prevent drying. Spray 1 sheet with nonstick spray; fold in half crosswise and spray again. Place in the pie pan, sprayed side down, allowing part of the sheet to hang over the edge of the pan. Repeat with the remaining sheets, overlapping slightly in the pan to cover the bottom completely. Spoon the broccoli-cheese mixture into the pie pan.

In a small bowl, combine the egg substitute, egg, and spices; pour over the broccoli-cheese mixture. Sprinkle with the remaining 1/4 cup cheese. Fold the phyllo over the filling; spray with nonstick cooking spray. Bake 35 to 40 minutes, or until the filling is set and the phyllo is golden. Serve immediately.

Fresh Herb Crepes

1 CUP ALL-PURPOSE FLOUR

1 CUP SKIM MILK

1 PACKET BUTTER BUDS MIX, LIQUEFIED

1/2 CUP LIQUID EGG SUBSTITUTE

1 TABLESPOON MINCED FRESH HERBS, SUCH AS PARSLEY, CHIVES, OR TARRAGON

In a medium bowl, combine all the ingredients. Beat with an electric mixer or whisk until smooth. Refrigerate 1 hour. Spray a 6-inch nonstick skillet with nonstick cooking spray. Heat over medium-high heat. Pour about 2 tablespoons batter into the skillet, swirling to spread the batter. Cook about 2 minutes, or until cooked on bottom. Flip and cook 45 seconds. Stack the crepes between sheets of wax paper to prevent sticking. Extra crepes may be frozen in a plastic freezer bag. Thaw at room temperature.

TIP: Fresh herbs can be stored several days in the refrigerator. After rinsing, wrap in paper toweling and place in a plastic bag. The towel absorbs the excess moisture and keeps the herbs fresh.

YIELD:
18 crepes
(18 servings)

**PER SERVING
(1 CREPE):**

35 calories

2 g protein

6 g carbohydrate

<1 g fat

0 g saturated fat

0 mg cholesterol

45 mg sodium

**DIABETIC
EXCHANGE:**

1/2 starch/bread
exchange

Asparagus-Mushroom Crepes

YIELD:
6 crepes
(6 servings)

**PER SERVING
(1 CREPE):**

70 calories

4 g protein

12 g carbohydrate

1 g fat

0 g saturated fat

0 mg cholesterol

150 mg sodium

**DIABETIC
EXCHANGES:**

1/2 starch/bread
exchange

1 vegetable
exchange

24 FRESH THIN ASPARAGUS SPEARS (ABOUT 12 OUNCES) OR
ONE PACKAGE (10 OUNCES) FROZEN PETITE ASPARAGUS SPEARS

3 CUPS SLICED FRESH MUSHROOMS (ABOUT 8 OUNCES)

1 PACKET BUTTER BUDS MIX, LIQUEFIED, DIVIDED

2 TABLESPOONS DRY SHERRY

1 LARGE GARLIC CLOVE, MINCED

1-1/2 TEASPOONS FRESH MINCED ROSEMARY OR
1/2 TEASPOON DRIED

1/2 CUP SKIM MILK

2 TEASPOONS CORNSTARCH

1/8 TEASPOON FRESHLY GROUND BLACK PEPPER, OR TO TASTE

6 FRESH HERB CREPES (PAGE 57)

Preheat the oven to 350°F.

Cook the asparagus in unsalted simmering water until tender (or cook according to package directions without salt); drain and set aside. In a medium skillet over medium heat, cook the mushrooms, 1/4 cup Butter Buds, sherry, garlic, and rosemary, covered, 3 to 5 minutes, or until the mushrooms are tender. In a small bowl, combine the milk and cornstarch; stir in the remaining 1/4 cup Butter Buds and pepper. Add to the mushrooms; cook, stirring until thickened. Remove from the heat.

To assemble the crepes: Place 4 asparagus on each crepe. Top with some of the mushroom mixture. Fold over and place in a baking dish that has been sprayed with nonstick cooking spray. Bake, covered, 15 minutes, or until heated through.

TIP: Place filled crepes in a single layer in a freezer container. Reheat in 350°F oven 20 to 30 minutes, or until heated through.

Spinach Cheese Crepes

1/2 CUP CHOPPED ONION

1 LARGE GARLIC CLOVE, MINCED

4 TABLESPOONS LIQUEFIED BUTTER BUDS MIX, DIVIDED

1 PACKAGE (10 OUNCES) FROZEN CHOPPED SPINACH

1/2 CUP PART-SKIM RICOTTA CHEESE

3 TABLESPOONS FAT-FREE PARMESAN CHEESE TOPPING

1/4 TEASPOON OREGANO

1/8 TEASPOON EACH: BLACK PEPPER AND
GROUND NUTMEG

8 FRESH HERB CREPES (PAGE 57)

LEMON BUTTER SAUCE, OPTIONAL (PAGE 84)

Preheat the oven to 350°F.

In a medium skillet over medium heat, cook the onion and garlic in 2 tablespoons Butter Buds until softened. Stir in the spinach and cook until dry; remove from the heat. Stir in the remaining 2 tablespoons Butter Buds, cheeses, oregano, pepper, and nutmeg.

To assemble the crepes: Place 1/4 cup filling on each crepe. Fold over and place in a baking dish that has been sprayed with nonstick cooking spray. Bake, covered, 15 minutes, or until heated through. Serve with Lemon Butter Sauce, if desired.

TIP: For a do-it-yourself party, let guests design their own crepes by choosing from a selection of prepared fillings. Bake as directed and enjoy!

YIELD:
8 crepes
(8 servings)

**PER SERVING
(1 CREPE):**

80 calories

5 g protein

12 g carbohydrate

2 g fat

1 g saturated fat

5 mg cholesterol

150 mg sodium

**DIABETIC
EXCHANGES:**

1/4 low-fat milk exchange

1/2 starch/bread exchange

1/2 vegetable exchange

YIELD:
10 slices
(10 servings)

**PER SERVING
(1 SLICE):**

107 calories

3 g protein

19 g carbohydrate

3 g fat

<1 g saturated fat

0 mg cholesterol

248 mg sodium

**DIABETIC
EXCHANGES:**

1 starch/bread
exchange

1/2 fat exchange

Garlic Bread

1 LOAF (12 TO 16 OUNCES) FRENCH OR ITALIAN BREAD

1 TABLESPOON OLIVE OIL

1/3 CUP BASIC GARLIC SAUCE (PAGE 86)

PAPRIKA OR OREGANO, TO TASTE

Cut bread in half lengthwise. Stir olive oil into Basic Garlic Sauce; spread on both halves of bread. Sprinkle with paprika and oregano, if desired. Bake at 400°F 10 to 12 minutes or broil 3 to 4 inches from heat source for 2 to 3 minutes, or until golden. Cut into 10 slices.

TIP: Garlic has been found to be a healthful addition to the diet and may help promote heart health.

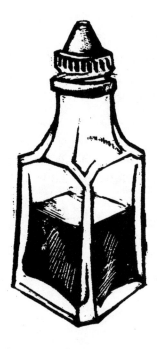

Bread Dough Pizza Crusts

1 LOAF (16 OUNCES) FROZEN WHITE BREAD DOUGH

1 TABLESPOON CORNMEAL

2 TABLESPOONS LIQUEFIED BUTTER BUDS MIX

1 TABLESPOON OLIVE OIL

**1 TEASPOON SALT-FREE GARLIC-AND-HERB
SEASONING BLEND**

Thaw the bread dough. On a lightly floured surface, divide the dough into 8 pieces. Cover; let the dough rest for 10 minutes.

Spray 2 cookie sheets with nonstick cooking spray; sprinkle with cornmeal. Using your hands, flatten each piece of dough into a 6-inch circle; place on the prepared pans.

Preheat the oven to 425°F.

In a small dish, combine the Butter Buds, oil, and seasoning blend. Brush the mixture on the dough rounds. Bake 7 minutes. Remove the pans to wire racks to cool.

YIELD:
8 bread dough
pizza crusts
(8 servings)

**PER SERVING
(1 CRUST):**

170 calories

5 g protein

31 g carbohydrate

3 g fat

<1 g saturated fat

0 mg cholesterol

330 mg sodium

**DIABETIC
EXCHANGES:**

2 starch/bread
exchanges

1/2 fat exchange

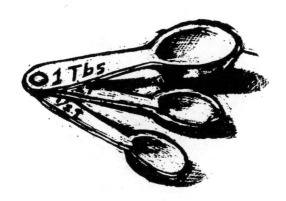

YIELD:

8 pizzas
(8 servings)

**PER SERVING
(1 PIZZA):**

220 calories

9 g protein

34 g carbohydrates

6 g fat

2 g saturated fat

10 mg cholesterol

440 mg sodium

**DIABETIC
EXCHANGES:**

1/2 low-fat milk
exchange

2 starch/bread
exchanges

1/2 fat exchange

Mushroom Pizza

3 CUPS SLICED FRESH MUSHROOMS (ABOUT 8 OUNCES)

2 TABLESPOONS FINELY CHOPPED ONION

1 SMALL GARLIC CLOVE, MINCED, OPTIONAL

3 TABLESPOONS LIQUEFIED BUTTER BUDS MIX

1/2 CUP BASIC MARINARA SAUCE (PAGE 94)

8 BREAD DOUGH PIZZA CRUSTS (PAGE 61)

1 CUP (4 OUNCES) SHREDDED PART-SKIM MOZZARELLA CHEESE

DRIED BASIL AND OREGANO, CRUMBLED

Preheat the oven to 450°F.

In a medium skillet over medium heat, cook the mushrooms, onion, and garlic in Butter Buds 5 to 7 minutes, or until softened and most of the liquid has evaporated; remove from the heat. Spread about 1 tablespoon Basic Marinara Sauce on each prepared crust. Spoon equal amounts of mushroom mixture on each crust. Top each pizza with about 2 tablespoons cheese and sprinkle with basil and oregano. Return to the oven and bake 12 to 15 minutes, or until the crust is golden.

Broccoli-Ricotta Pizza

1/4 CUP FINELY CHOPPED ONION

1 GARLIC CLOVE, MINCED

2 TABLESPOONS LIQUEFIED BUTTER BUDS MIX

1/2 CUP PART-SKIM RICOTTA CHEESE

DRIED BASIL AND OREGANO, CRUMBLED

8 BREAD DOUGH PIZZA CRUSTS (PAGE 61)

2 CUPS COOKED BROCCOLI FLORETS

2 TABLESPOONS GRATED PARMESAN CHEESE

Preheat the oven to 450°F.

In a small skillet over medium heat, cook the onion and garlic in Butter Buds about 3 minutes, or until softened. Remove from the heat; stir in the ricotta cheese. Season to taste with basil and oregano. Spread about 1 tablespoon filling on each prepared pizza crust. Place equal amounts of cooked broccoli on each crust. Sprinkle with Parmesan cheese. Bake 12 to 15 minutes, or until the crust is golden.

YIELD:
8 pizzas
(8 servings)

**PER SERVING
(1 PIZZA):**

215 calories

9 g protein

35 g carbohydrate

5 g fat

1 g saturated fat

5 mg cholesterol

405 mg sodium

**DIABETIC
EXCHANGES:**

1/2 low-fat milk
exchange

1-1/2 starch/bread
exchanges

1 vegetable
exchange

1/2 fat exchange

YIELD:
8 pizzas
(8 servings)

**PER SERVING
(1 PIZZA):**

215 calories

9 g protein

36 g carbohydrate

4 g fat

<1 g saturated fat

5 mg cholesterol

440 mg sodium

**DIABETIC
EXCHANGES:**

1/2 low-fat milk
exchange

1-1/2 starch/bread
exchanges

1 vegetable
exchange

Pepper Medley Pizza

---

1 LARGE GREEN BELL PEPPER, CUT INTO THIN STRIPS
1 LARGE RED BELL PEPPER, CUT INTO THIN STRIPS
1 LARGE ONION, THINLY SLICED
1/4 CUP LIQUEFIED BUTTER BUDS MIX
1/8 TEASPOON CRUSHED HOT RED PEPPER FLAKES
8 BREAD DOUGH PIZZA CRUSTS (PAGE 61)
1 CUP (4 OUNCES) SHREDDED PART-SKIM MOZZARELLA CHEESE
DRIED BASIL AND OREGANO, CRUMBLED

Preheat the oven to 450°F.

Spray a large nonstick skillet with nonstick cooking spray and heat over medium-high heat. Add the peppers and onion; cook, stirring constantly, 3 minutes. Add the Butter Buds and crushed red pepper flakes. Reduce the heat to medium and cook, covered, 3 minutes. Uncover; cook an additional 3 minutes, or until most of the liquid has evaporated. Spoon equal amounts of the mixture on the prepared pizza crusts. Top each pizza with about 2 tablespoons cheese. Sprinkle with basil and oregano. Bake 12 to 15 minutes, or until the cheese is melted and crust is golden.

Soups and Salads

Soups and salads are perfect to build meals around. Sometimes, with heartier versions, all that is needed is some good bread. Cool down with our tasty Couscous Salad, Crunchy Potato Salad, or Mixed Vegetable Slaw. Warm up with our super Corn and Crab Chowder, Beef-Barley Soup with Mushrooms, or Cream of Fresh Tomato Soup. All of these selections are sure to provide a taste bud sensation!

Cream of Fresh Tomato Soup

YIELD:
4 cups (4 servings)

**PER SERVING
(1 CUP):**

105 calories

5 g protein

21 g carbohydrate

2 g fat

1 g saturated fat

5 mg cholesterol

205 mg sodium

**DIABETIC
EXCHANGE:**

1/2 low-fat milk
exchange

1/2 starch/bread
exchange

2 vegetable
exchanges

1-1/2 POUNDS TOMATOES, PEELED

1/4 CUP CHOPPED ONION

1/4 CUP FRESH PARSLEY

1 SMALL CLOVE GARLIC

1/4 TEASPOON DRIED BASIL

1-1/2 CUPS 1% FAT MILK

2 TABLESPOONS ALL-PURPOSE FLOUR

1 PACKET BUTTER BUDS MIX, LIQUEFIED

1/4 TEASPOON SAGE

FRESHLY GROUND BLACK PEPPER, TO TASTE

CHOPPED FRESH PARSLEY, FOR GARNISH

Cut tomatoes in half crosswise. Place a colander over a bowl. Gently squeeze tomato halves over the colander to remove seeds, and reserve the juice. Discard the seeds; pour the juice into a medium saucepan. In a food processor, combine the tomatoes, onion, parsley, garlic, and basil. Process until the tomatoes are chopped. Pour into a saucepan. Over high heat, bring the mixture to a boil. Reduce heat to medium; cook 15 minutes. In a 2-cup measure, combine milk and flour. Stir in the Butter Buds. In a small saucepan over medium heat, cook the milk mixture, stirring constantly, until it is thickened and smooth. Slowly stir it into the tomato mixture. Add sage and pepper to taste. Heat through. Garnish with chopped parsley.

TIP: To peel tomatoes, drop in boiling water for 30 seconds. Transfer immediately to a bowl of cold water and peel.

Beef-Barley Soup with Mushrooms

8 OUNCES BEEF ROUND STEAK, DICED

1 LARGE ONION, CHOPPED (1 CUP)

1 LARGE GARLIC CLOVE, MINCED

4 PACKETS REDUCED-SODIUM BEEF FLAVOR
INSTANT BROTH AND SEASONING

5 CUPS HOT WATER

1/2 CUP DRY SHERRY

2 TABLESPOONS BUTTER BUDS SPRINKLES

1 TABLESPOON REDUCED-SODIUM
WORCESTERSHIRE SAUCE

1-1/2 CUPS SLICED CARROTS

3 CUPS SLICED FRESH MUSHROOMS (ABOUT 8 OUNCES)

1/2 CUP UNCOOKED PEARL BARLEY

1 BAY LEAF

1/2 TEASPOON DRIED THYME, CRUMBLED

FRESHLY GROUND BLACK PEPPER, TO TASTE

YIELD:
6 cups (8 servings)

**PER SERVING
(3/4 CUP):**

140 calories

12 g protein

17 g carbohydrate

3 g fat

1 g saturated fat

25 mg cholesterol

115 mg sodium

**DIABETIC
EXCHANGES:**

1 starch/bread
exchange

1 vegetable
exchange

1 lean meat
exchange

Spray a 3- or 4-quart saucepan with nonstick cooking spray and heat over medium-high heat. Add the beef, onion, and garlic and cook until the beef is browned. Stir the instant broth into the water; add 1 cup to the saucepan with the sherry, Butter Buds, and Worcestershire sauce. Reduce the heat; cover and simmer 20 minutes. Add the remaining broth, carrots, mushrooms, barley, bay leaf, thyme, and pepper to the saucepan. Simmer, covered, 45 minutes, or until the barley is tender.

Corn and Crab Chowder

YIELD:
5 cups
(approximately
6-1/2 servings)

**PER SERVING
(3/4 CUP):**

125 calories

8 g protein

20 g carbohydrate

2 g fat

<1 g saturated fat

25 mg cholesterol

160 mg sodium

**DIABETIC
EXCHANGES:**

1 starch/bread
exchange

1 lean meat
exchange

**2 EARS FRESH CORN ON THE COB OR 1 CUP CANNED OR
FROZEN (THAWED) CORN**

3 TABLESPOONS LIQUEFIED BUTTER BUDS

3/4 CUP EACH, FINELY CHOPPED: CARROTS, CELERY, AND ONION

1/4 CUP FINELY CHOPPED RED BELL PEPPER

2 MEDIUM POTATOES, PEELED AND DICED (6 OUNCES EACH)

1 CAN (10 OUNCES) ALL-NATURAL CLAM JUICE

1 CUP 1% FAT MILK

1 TABLESPOON ALL-PURPOSE FLOUR

1/4 TEASPOON DRIED THYME, CRUMBLED

FRESHLY GROUND BLACK PEPPER, TO TASTE

1 CAN (6-1/2 OUNCES) CRABMEAT, DRAINED AND RINSED

3 TABLESPOONS HALF-AND-HALF

If using fresh corn on the cob, place the corn in unsalted boiling water to cover; remove from the heat, cover, and let stand 5 minutes. Drain and cool. Cut kernels from the cob; set aside. Spray a medium-size saucepan with nonstick cooking spray. Add the Butter Buds and heat over medium heat. Add the carrots, celery, onion, and red pepper. Cook, stirring, 3 minutes. Add the potatoes; toss to coat. Add clam juice and bring to a boil. Reduce the heat, cover, and simmer 10 minutes, or until the potatoes are tender. Stir in the corn. In a small saucepan, combine the milk, flour, thyme, and pepper. Over medium heat, cook, stirring constantly, until thickened. Gradually stir the milk mixture into the vegetables. Add the crabmeat and half-and-half. Cook until heated through.

Tortellini Salad

5 CUPS ASSORTED FRESH VEGETABLES: BROCCOLI AND
CAULIFLOWER FLORETS AND JULIENNE-CUT CARROTS

1 PACKAGE (9 OUNCES) FRESH CHEESE TORTELLINI

1 TABLESPOON BUTTER BUDS SPRINKLES

1 CUP HERB VINAIGRETTE (PAGE 89) WITH 2 TEASPOONS
ONION-HERB MIXTURE STIRRED IN

1 GREEN, RED, OR YELLOW BELL PEPPER, CUT INTO STRIPS

1/2 CUP TORN FRESH SPINACH OR WATERCRESS

FRESHLY GROUND BLACK PEPPER, TO TASTE

ADDITIONAL FRESH SPINACH LEAVES OR WATERCRESS,
FOR GARNISH

YIELD:
8 cups (8 servings)

**PER SERVING
(1 CUP):**

160 calories

7 g protein

24 g carbohydrate

4 g fat

1 g saturated fat

15 mg cholesterol

250 mg sodium

**DIABETIC
EXCHANGES:**

1-1/2 starch/bread
exchanges

1 vegetable
exchange

In a large pot of boiling water, blanch the broccoli, cauliflower, and carrots for 2 minutes. With a slotted spoon, transfer immediately to a large bowl of cold water. Drain and return to the bowl. Add the tortellini to the boiling water; cook according to package directions but without salt. Drain and add to the blanched vegetables. Add the Butter Buds and toss. Add the Herb Vinaigrette, bell pepper, spinach or watercress, and black pepper; toss until well blended. Cover and refrigerate several hours or overnight for the flavors to blend. Serve the salad on a platter lined with spinach leaves or watercress. The salad will keep in the refrigerator for 2 to 3 days.

TIP: When this salad sits overnight, the tortellini has time to absorb the vinaigrette, making it tender and flavorful. It's worth the wait!

YIELD:
6 cups (12 servings)

PER SERVING (1/2 CUP):

70 calories

3 g protein

13 g carbohydrate

1 g fat

0 g saturated fat

0 mg cholesterol

70 mg sodium

DIABETIC EXCHANGE:

1 starch/bread exchange

Crunchy Potato Salad

1-1/2 POUNDS RED-SKINNED POTATOES

1 CUP CHOPPED CELERY

1/2 CUP CHOPPED GREEN BELL PEPPER

**1/2 CUP JULIENNE-CUT RADISHES
(APPROXIMATELY 6 RADISHES)**

1/2 CUP CHOPPED RED ONION

2 LARGE HARD-COOKED EGG WHITES, CHOPPED

1/2 CUP NONFAT SOUR CREAM

2 TABLESPOONS REDUCED-CALORIE MAYONNAISE

3 TABLESPOONS RED WINE VINEGAR

1 TABLESPOON BUTTER BUDS SPRINKLES

2 PACKETS SWEET 'N LOW

3/4 TEASPOON CELERY SEED

1/2 TEASPOON DRY MUSTARD

1/4 TEASPOON EACH: SALT AND FRESHLY GROUND PEPPER

Cook the potatoes in a large pot of boiling water until tender; drain. When cool enough to handle, cut into chunks and transfer to a large bowl. Add the celery, bell pepper, radishes, onion, and egg whites. In a small bowl, combine the remaining ingredients; add to the potato mixture and toss until well blended. Cover and refrigerate several hours for the flavors to blend. Stir well before serving. This salad will keep several days in the refrigerator.

TIP: Fresh lemon juice will take away onion scent from hands.

Couscous Salad

1/3 CUP BASIC GARLIC SAUCE (PAGE 86)

1-1/4 CUPS WATER

3/4 CUP UNCOOKED QUICK-COOKING COUSCOUS

3/4 CUP EACH, FINELY CHOPPED: CARROTS AND CELERY

1/4 CUP FINELY CHOPPED ONION

3 TABLESPOONS FAT-FREE PARMESAN CHEESE TOPPING

2 TABLESPOONS EACH: LEMON JUICE AND RED WINE VINEGAR

1 TABLESPOON OLIVE OIL

FRESHLY GROUND BLACK PEPPER, TO TASTE

To prepare in the microwave: Prepare the Basic Garlic Sauce and place in a 1-quart microwave-safe casserole. Add the water. Cook, covered, on 100% power for 2 to 3 minutes, or until the mixture comes to a rolling boil. Stir in the couscous; cover and set aside 5 minutes, or until the couscous is tender. Add the remaining ingredients to the cooked couscous. Cover and refrigerate several hours for the flavors to blend.

To prepare on the stove: Prepare the Basic Garlic Sauce and place in a medium saucepan. Add water and bring to a boil over medium-high heat. Remove from the heat and stir in couscous. Cover and set aside 5 minutes, or until the couscous is tender. Add the remaining ingredients to the cooked couscous. Cover and refrigerate several hours for the flavors to blend.

SERVING SUGGESTION: Cut a medium-size zucchini into 1-1/2-inch pieces. Using a melon baller, hollow out each piece, leaving the bottom intact; fill with about 1 tablespoon couscous salad. Cut a thin slice from the bottom of ripe plum tomatoes so they stand upright; cut off the tops. Using a melon baller, scoop out the seeds and pulp; fill with 1 to 2 tablespoons couscous salad. Serve as an appetizer or garnish for main dish meals.

YIELD:
4 cups (8 servings)

**PER SERVING
(1/2 CUP):**

100 calories

3 g protein

19 g carbohydrate

2 g fat

<1 g saturated fat

0 mg cholesterol

110 mg sodium

**DIABETIC
EXCHANGE:**

1 starch/bread
exchange

Mixed Vegetable Slaw

YIELD:
4 cups (8 servings)

PER SERVING (1/2 CUP):

45 calories

1 g protein

9 g carbohydrate

1 g fat

<1 g saturated fat

<1 mg cholesterol

100 mg sodium

DIABETIC EXCHANGE:

1 vegetable exchange

3 CUPS SHREDDED GREEN CABBAGE

2 CUPS SHREDDED RED CABBAGE

1 CUP SHREDDED CARROT

1/4 CUP CHOPPED ONION

1 PACKET BUTTER BUDS MIX, LIQUEFIED

1/3 CUP NONFAT SOUR CREAM

3 TABLESPOONS CIDER VINEGAR

2 TABLESPOONS REDUCED-CALORIE MAYONNAISE

1/2 TEASPOON CELERY SEED

1 PACKET SWEET 'N LOW

1/4 TEASPOON DRIED OREGANO, CRUMBLED

FRESHLY GROUND BLACK PEPPER, TO TASTE

ALFALFA SPROUTS, FOR GARNISH (OPTIONAL)

In a large bowl, combine the first 4 ingredients. In a small bowl, stir together the remaining ingredients except the alfalfa sprouts. Pour over the vegetables and toss to coat. Cover and refrigerate several hours for the flavors to blend. Garnish with alfalfa sprouts, if desired.

A Harvest of Vegetables

Move over, main dishes, because here comes a selection of vegetable dishes that will excite the whole family. You'll never look at vegetables the same way again.

Gingered Carrots and Snow Peas

3 LARGE CARROTS

6 OUNCES FRESH SNOW PEAS

3/4 CUP FRESHLY SQUEEZED ORANGE JUICE

2 TABLESPOONS LIGHT BROWN SUGAR

1-1/2 TEASPOONS BUTTER BUDS SPRINKLES

1-1/2 TEASPOONS CORNSTARCH

1 TEASPOON GRATED FRESH GINGER

1/2 TEASPOON GRATED ORANGE PEEL

1/8 TEASPOON SALT

1 TABLESPOON THINLY SLICED SCALLIONS, FOR GARNISH

Peel the carrots; slice diagonally 1/2 inch thick. In a medium pot of boiling water, cook the carrots 8 minutes. Add the snow peas; cook an additional 2 minutes. Drain. Meanwhile, in a small saucepan, combine the remaining ingredients, except the scallions. Cook over medium heat, stirring constantly, 1 to 2 minutes, or until the mixture is thickened and bubbly. Stir in the drained carrots and snow peas; cook until heated through. Garnish with the sliced scallions.

TIP: Carrots are an excellent source of beta carotene, an antioxidant nutrient that may help protect against a number of chronic diseases.

YIELD:
3 cups (6 servings)

**PER SERVING
(1/2 CUP):**

65 calories

1 g protein

15 g carbohydrate

<1 g fat

<1 g saturated fat

0 mg cholesterol

80 mg sodium

**DIABETIC
EXCHANGES:**

1/2 fruit exchange

1 vegetable exchange

Savory Artichokes and Mushrooms

2 PACKAGES (10 OUNCES EACH) FROZEN ARTICHOKES

1/2 CUP DRY SHERRY

1/4 CUP LIQUEFIED BUTTER BUDS MIX

1 TABLESPOON PARSLEY FLAKES

1 TABLESPOON MINCED SHALLOTS

1 GARLIC CLOVE, MINCED

2 TEASPOONS LEMON JUICE

1/2 TEASPOON DRY MUSTARD

1/2 TEASPOON DRIED TARRAGON

FRESHLY GROUND BLACK PEPPER, TO TASTE

1 PACKAGE (12 OUNCES) FRESH WHOLE MUSHROOMS

2 TEASPOONS CORNSTARCH DISSOLVED IN
1-1/2 TABLESPOONS COLD WATER

Cook the artichokes according to package directions but without salt; drain and set aside. In a large skillet, combine the next 9 ingredients. Bring to a boil over medium heat. Rinse the mushrooms and trim the bottom of the stems. Cut large mushrooms in half; add to the skillet. Reduce the heat, cover, and simmer 3 minutes. Add the dissolved cornstarch; cook, stirring constantly, 1 to 2 minutes or until thickened and bubbly. Stir in the artichokes and cook until heated through.

YIELD:
4-1/2 cups
(6 servings)

**PER SERVING
(3/4 CUP):**

75 calories

5 g protein

15 g carbohydrate

1 g fat

0 g saturated fat

0 mg cholesterol

140 mg sodium

**DIABETIC
EXCHANGES:**

2 vegetable
exchanges

BB

YIELD:
8 cups (16 servings)

**PER SERVING
(1/2 CUP):**

45 calories

2 g protein

8 g carbohydrate

1 g fat

<1 g saturated fat

0 mg cholesterol

40 mg sodium

**DIABETIC
EXCHANGE:**

1 vegetable
exchange

Ratatouille

1 TABLESPOON OLIVE OIL

1 LARGE ONION, DICED (ABOUT 2 CUPS)

1 LARGE GARLIC CLOVE, MINCED

1 PACKET BUTTER BUDS MIX, LIQUEFIED

1 MEDIUM EGGPLANT, CUT INTO CHUNKS (ABOUT 5 CUPS)

1 LARGE GREEN BELL PEPPER, CUT INTO CHUNKS
(ABOUT 1-1/2 CUPS)

3 MEDIUM ZUCCHINI, CUT INTO 1-INCH PIECES
(ABOUT 6 CUPS)

2 TEASPOONS DRIED OREGANO, CRUMBLED

1/2 TEASPOON DRIED THYME, CRUMBLED

2 PACKETS SWEET 'N LOW

FRESHLY GROUND BLACK PEPPER, TO TASTE

2 LARGE TOMATOES, PEELED AND CUT INTO WEDGES

In a large saucepan over medium heat, heat the oil. When hot, add the onion and garlic; cook, stirring, 3 to 4 minutes. Add the Butter Buds, eggplant, and green pepper; cook, stirring frequently, about 5 minutes. Stir in the zucchini, oregano, thyme, Sweet 'N Low, and pepper. Bring to a boil; reduce the heat and cook, partially covered, 15 to 20 minutes, or until the vegetables are tender. Stir in the tomatoes; cook an additional 5 minutes. Serve hot, or refrigerate and serve cold.

SERVING SUGGESTIONS: Serve over cooked pasta as a main dish; sprinkle with grated Parmesan cheese or fat-free grated Parmesan Italian topping. Stir in drained and rinsed canned chickpeas or white beans; serve over cooked rice or a baked potato.

Dilled Cucumbers

2 MEDIUM CUCUMBERS, PEELED AND SLICED (4 CUPS)

1 LARGE ONION, SLICED (ABOUT 1-1/2 CUPS)

2 TABLESPOONS CHOPPED FRESH DILL

2 PACKETS SWEET 'N LOW

1/2 CUP DISTILLED WHITE VINEGAR

GENEROUS AMOUNT OF FRESHLY GROUND BLACK PEPPER

In a medium bowl, combine the cucumbers, onion, and dill. In a 1-cup measure, stir the Sweet 'N Low into the vinegar to dissolve. Add to the cucumber mixture and season with pepper. Cover and refrigerate several hours or overnight.

TIP: To seed cucumbers (if desired), cut in half lengthwise. With a melon baller or the tip of a teaspoon, scrape out the seeds and pulp; discard.

YIELD:
5 cups (10 servings)

PER SERVING (1/2 CUP):

20 calories

1 g protein

4 g carbohydrate

<1 g fat

0 g saturated fat

0 mg cholesterol

5 mg sodium

DIABETIC EXCHANGE:

Free exchange

Marinated Vegetables

YIELD:
7 cups (14 servings)

PER SERVING
(1/2 CUP):

30 calories

1 g protein

7 g carbohydrate

<1 g fat

<1 g saturated fat

0 mg cholesterol

75 mg sodium

DIABETIC
EXCHANGE:

1 vegetable
exchange

**2 CUPS FRESH GREEN BEANS OR WAXED BEANS,
CUT IN HALF (8 OUNCES)**

3 CUPS FRESH BROCCOLI FLORETS (8 OUNCES)

2-1/2 CUPS FRESH CAULIFLOWER FLORETS (8 OUNCES)

3 MEDIUM CARROTS, SLICED THIN (1 CUP)

1 PACKET BUTTER BUDS MIX, LIQUEFIED

1/2 CUP CHOPPED RED ONION

1/2 CUP RED WINE VINEGAR

1 TABLESPOON MINCED FRESH DILL

1 GARLIC CLOVE, MINCED

1/8 TEASPOON SALT

FRESHLY GROUND BLACK PEPPER, TO TASTE

In a large pot, heat water to boiling. Blanch the beans, broccoli, cauliflower, and carrots for 2 minutes. Transfer immediately to a large bowl of cold water. Drain and return to the bowl. In a small bowl, combine the remaining ingredients, stirring to blend well. Pour over the vegetables and toss to coat. Cover and refrigerate several hours for the flavors to blend. Stir before serving. The vegetables will keep several days in the refrigerator.

Garlic Stuffed Mushrooms

1 PACKAGE (12 OUNCES) FRESH WHOLE MUSHROOMS

1/3 CUP BASIC GARLIC SAUCE (PAGE 86)

1/4 CUP FINELY CHOPPED ONION

1 TEASPOON LEMON JUICE

1 TEASPOON DRIED SAVORY, CRUMBLED

1/3 CUP PLAIN DRY BREAD CRUMBS

1/2 CUP (2 OUNCES) SHREDDED REDUCED-FAT MOZZARELLA CHEESE

Preheat the oven to 400°F.

Rinse the mushrooms to remove any dirt. Trim the bottom of the stems; remove from the caps and chop finely.

In a medium-size skillet over medium heat, cook the Basic Garlic Sauce, chopped mushroom stems, onion, lemon juice, and savory for 5 minutes. Stir in the bread crumbs and remove from the heat. Cool slightly. Stir in the cheese.

Place the mushroom caps in a shallow baking pan or cookie sheet. Fill the caps with the stuffing mixture. Bake 15 minutes, or until the mushrooms are tender.

YIELD:
16 to 20 pieces, depending on mushroom size (8 to 10 servings)

PER SERVING (2 MUSHROOMS):

50 calories

4 g protein

7 g carbohydrate

2 g fat

1 g saturated fat

40 mg cholesterol

155 mg sodium

DIABETIC EXCHANGE:

1/2 starch/bread exchange

Herb Stuffing

YIELD:
3 cups (6 servings)

PER SERVING (1/2 CUP):

85 calories

4 g protein

15 g carbohydrate

<1 g fat

0 g saturated fat

0 mg cholesterol

230 mg sodium

DIABETIC EXCHANGES:

1/2 starch/bread exchange

1 vegetable exchange

1/2 CUP EACH, FINELY CHOPPED: CARROTS, CELERY, ONIONS, GREEN BELL PEPPERS, AND ZUCCHINI

1 CAN (10-1/2 OUNCES) REDUCED-SODIUM CHICKEN BROTH

1 TABLESPOON BUTTER BUDS SPRINKLES

1 TEASPOON GROUND THYME

1/2 TEASPOON GROUND SAGE

FRESHLY GROUND BLACK PEPPER, TO TASTE

9 SLICES REDUCED-CALORIE WHOLE WHEAT BREAD, CUBED

Spray a large nonstick skillet with nonstick cooking spray and heat over medium heat. Add the carrots, celery, onion, bell peppers, and zucchini; cook 5 minutes, stirring constantly. Add the chicken broth, Butter Buds, thyme, sage, and black pepper; bring to a boil. Reduce the heat, cover, and simmer 5 minutes. Add the bread cubes and continue cooking, stirring until the mixture is blended.

Signature Sauces

Start with a plain piece of broiled meat, poached fish, or baked poultry; steamed vegetables; and rice, pasta, or potatoes. Add one of our sauces, such as a Tarragon Sauce, Basic Garlic Sauce, or Velouté Sauce, and you'll create a signature meal that will surprise even yourself.

Sweet-and-Sour Sauce

YIELD:
3/4 cup (6 servings)

**PER SERVING
(2
TABLESPOONS):**

15 calories

<1 g protein

3 g carbohydrate

<1 g fat

<1 g saturated fat

0 mg cholesterol

40 mg sodium

**DIABETIC
EXCHANGE:**

Free exchange

1/4 CUP MINCED CARROT

1/4 CUP MINCED GREEN BELL PEPPER

1 LARGE GARLIC CLOVE, MINCED

1/2 CUP REDUCED-SODIUM CHICKEN BROTH

3 TABLESPOONS WHITE VINEGAR

1 TEASPOON REDUCED-SODIUM SOY SAUCE

1 TABLESPOON CORNSTARCH DISSOLVED IN
2 TABLESPOONS COLD WATER

2 PACKETS SWEET 'N LOW, OR TO TASTE

Spray a small nonstick skillet with nonstick cooking spray and heat over medium-high heat. Add the carrot, green pepper, and garlic; cook, stirring about 3 minutes, or until the vegetables begin to brown slightly. Stir in the broth, vinegar, and soy sauce; bring to a boil. Boil 1 minute. Add the cornstarch mixture and cook, stirring constantly until sauce thickens. Stir in the Sweet 'N Low. Brush over chicken, pork, or vegetables or use as a dip with egg rolls, chicken fingers, or ribs. The recipe may be doubled.

TIP: One large garlic clove yields approximately 1 teaspoon minced garlic. Minced garlic can be stored in an airtight container in the refrigerator for 1 to 2 days.

Barbecue Sauce

1 CAN (8 OUNCES) REDUCED-SODIUM TOMATO SAUCE

1 SMALL ONION, FINELY CHOPPED

2 TABLESPOONS CIDER VINEGAR

1 TABLESPOON LIGHT BROWN SUGAR

1 TABLESPOON REDUCED-SODIUM WORCESTERSHIRE SAUCE

1 TEASPOON CHILI POWDER

CAYENNE PEPPER, TO TASTE

1/3 CUP BASIC GARLIC SAUCE (PAGE 86)

Stir the first 7 ingredients into the Basic Garlic Sauce. Cook over low heat 20 minutes, or until slightly thickened. The sauce can be brushed on chicken, ribs, or any meat before barbecuing, or served on the side.

YIELD:
1-1/2 cups
(24 servings)

**PER SERVING
(1 TABLESPOON):**

10 calories

<1 g protein

3 g carbohydrate

<1 g fat

0 g saturated fat

0 mg cholesterol

30 mg sodium

DIABETIC EXCHANGE:

Free exchange

Lemon Butter Sauce

YIELD:
1/2 cup (8 servings)

PER SERVING
(1
TABLESPOON):

10 calories

0 g protein

3 g carbohydrate

0 g fat

0 g saturated fat

0 mg cholesterol

70 mg sodium

DIABETIC
EXCHANGE:

Free exchange

1/4 CUP WATER

2 TABLESPOONS LEMON JUICE, PREFERABLY FRESH

1 SHALLOT, MINCED (2 TABLESPOONS)

1-1/2 TABLESPOONS MINCED FRESH PARSLEY

1-1/2 TEASPOONS HERBES DE PROVENCE, FINES HERBES, OR YOUR FAVORITE HERB BLEND

1 PACKET BUTTER BUDS MIX, LIQUEFIED

In a small saucepan over medium-high heat, cook water, lemon juice, shallots, and herbs until reduced to 1 tablespoon. Gradually add the Butter Buds, stirring constantly, until the mixture comes to a boil; boil 1 minute. Strain if desired.

TIP: Lemon Butter Sauce goes great with seafood!

Tarragon Sauce

YIELD:
1/2 cup (8 servings)

PER SERVING
(1
TABLESPOON):

10 calories

<1 g protein

3 g carbohydrate

<1 g fat

0 g saturated fat

0 mg cholesterol

70 mg sodium

DIABETIC
EXCHANGE:

Free exchange

Replace the water and lemon juice with *2 tablespoons each: white wine and white wine vinegar.* Replace the herbs with *1 tablespoon fresh or 1-1/2 teaspoons dried tarragon.* Cook as directed.

Dill Sauce

Replace the water and lemon juice with *1/4 cup white wine.* Replace the herbs with *1-1/2 tablespoons minced fresh dill.* Cook as directed.

YIELD:
1/2 cup (8 servings)

PER SERVING (1 TABLESPOON):

10 calories

<1 g protein

3 g carbohydrate

<1 g fat

0 g saturated fat

0 mg cholesterol

70 mg sodium

DIABETIC EXCHANGE:

Free exchange

Basic Garlic Sauce

YIELD:
1/3 cup
(approximately 5
servings)

PER SERVING
(1
TABLESPOON):

10 calories

<1 g protein

3 g carbohydrate

0 g fat

0 g saturated fat

0 mg cholesterol

95 mg sodium

DIABETIC
EXCHANGE:

Free exchange

1 PACKET BUTTER BUDS MIX, DRY

1/4 CUP HOT WATER

1 LARGE GARLIC CLOVE, MINCED

1 TABLESPOON MINCED FRESH PARSLEY OR 1 TEASPOON DRIED

**1-1/2 TEASPOONS MINCED FRESH OREGANO OR
1/2 TEASPOON DRIED**

In a small bowl, dissolve the Butter Buds in the hot water; stir in the remaining ingredients. Brush on steak, chicken, or fish before broiling or serve on steamed vegetables. The recipe may be doubled.

Teriyaki Marinade

1/2 CUP REDUCED-SODIUM CHICKEN OR BEEF BROTH

1/2 CUP UNSWEETENED PINEAPPLE JUICE

1/4 CUP DRY SHERRY

2 TABLESPOONS REDUCED-SODIUM SOY SAUCE

1 LARGE GARLIC CLOVE, MINCED

1 TEASPOON GRATED FRESH GINGER

2 PACKETS SWEET 'N LOW

In a small saucepan over medium heat, bring all the ingredients to a boil. Boil 5 minutes. Remove from the heat and cool to room temperature.

NOTE: Teriyaki marinade can be made ahead of time and stored in the refrigerator. Two-thirds cup sauce is enough to marinate 1-1/2 pounds beef flank or round steak, 6 to 8 pieces of skinless chicken, or 1 to 1-1/2 pounds firm-fleshed fish or shrimp. Marinate several hours in the refrigerator. Grill or broil, as desired, using the marinade to baste the food as it cooks.

YIELD:
1 cup (8 servings)

PER SERVING (2 TABLESPOONS):

15 calories

<1 g protein

3 g carbohydrate

<1 g fat

0 g saturated fat

0 mg cholesterol

155 mg sodium

DIABETIC EXCHANGE:

Free exchange

Teriyaki Glaze

YIELD:
1 cup (16 servings)

PER SERVING
(1
TABLESPOON):

10 calories

<1 g protein

2 g carbohydrate

<1 g fat

0 g saturated fat

0 mg cholesterol

75 mg sodium

DIABETIC
EXCHANGE:

Free exchange

1 CUP TERIYAKI MARINADE (PAGE 87)

1 TABLESPOON CORNSTARCH DISSOLVED IN 3 TABLESPOONS COLD WATER

In a small saucepan, heat the sauce until hot; add the cornstarch mixture and cook, stirring constantly, 1 to 2 minutes, or until thickened and bubbly.

Herb Vinaigrette

1/3 CUP BALSAMIC VINEGAR

2 TABLESPOONS MINCED ONION OR SHALLOTS

1 GARLIC CLOVE, MINCED

1 TEASPOON EACH DRIED, CRUMBLED: BASIL, CHERVIL,
MARJORAM, AND THYME

1/4 TEASPOON EACH: SALT AND PEPPER

1 PACKET SWEET 'N LOW

2/3 CUP REDUCED-SODIUM CHICKEN BROTH

1 TEASPOON DIJON-STYLE MUSTARD

1 TABLESPOON OLIVE OIL

In a small bowl, stir together the vinegar, onion or shallots, garlic, herbs, salt, pepper, and Sweet 'N Low. Cover and refrigerate 24 hours. Strain the mixture, reserving the onion, garlic, and herbs. Whisk the broth and mustard into the vinegar. Whisk in the oil. For a more flavorful dressing, stir 2 teaspoons reserved onion-herb mixture back into the dressing. Refrigerate, covered, up to 1 week. Serve on salads and vegetables.

TIP: The reserved onion-herb mixture from the Herb Vinaigrette can be pureed with 3/4 cup nonfat cottage cheese and served as a dip with raw vegetables. Refrigerate at least 1 hour before serving. It makes about 3/4 cup, or six 2-tablespoon servings.

YIELD:
1 cup (16 servings)

**PER SERVING
(1 TABLESPOON):**

15 calories

<1 g protein

2 g carbohydrate

1 g fat

<1 g saturated fat

0 mg cholesterol

10 mg sodium

DIABETIC EXCHANGE:

Free exchange

Basic White Sauce

YIELD:
1 cup (16 servings)

PER SERVING
(1
TABLESPOON):

10 calories

1 g protein

3 g carbohydrate

<1 g fat

<1 g saturated fat

<1 mg cholesterol

15 mg sodium

DIABETIC
EXCHANGE:

Free exchange

B
B

1 CUP 2% FAT MILK

2 TABLESPOONS LIQUEFIED BUTTER BUDS MIX

1 TABLESPOON CORNSTARCH

In a small saucepan, whisk together all the ingredients. Cook over medium heat, stirring constantly, until the mixture comes to a boil and thickens. The recipe may be doubled.

NOTE: This is a basic unflavored sauce to be used as a base for other sauces. Season with pepper and nutmeg for a plain white sauce or, if a richer butter flavor is desired, additional dry Butter Buds Mix or Butter Buds Sprinkles may be added to the sauce.

TIPS: Adding a cornstarch mixture to a hot liquid produces a thicker sauce than when cornstarch is added to a cold liquid and brought to a boil to thicken. A cornstarch-thickened sauce must always come to a boil for thickening to occur.

Cream sauces made ahead can be held by pouring a thin layer of milk over the surface and covering with plastic wrap. Reheat over low heat.

TIPS: Cream sauces can be made in advance and refrigerated for two to three days. Before refrigerating pour a thin layer of milk over the surface and cover with plastic wrap. When ready to use sauce reheat over low heat.

Velouté Sauce

Replace the milk with *1 cup reduced-sodium chicken or beef broth*. Season to taste with *fresh or dried herbs**.

*NOTE: *Seasoning suggestions*

1/2 to 1   teaspoon salt-free garlic-and-herb seasoning blend (poultry, pasta, seafood, and meat)

2   teaspoons fresh or 1/2 teaspoon dried tarragon (poultry)

1/2 to 1   teaspoon dried fines herbes (poultry, seafood)

1/2 to 1   teaspoon Herbes de Provence (meat, poultry)

Mix together 1 tablespoon minced fresh parsley, 1 tablespoon red pepper, and 1/2 teaspoon minced fresh garlic (pasta, chicken, veal, and steamed fresh vegetables)

YIELD:
1 cup (8 servings)

PER SERVING (2 TABLESPOONS):

10 calories

<1 g protein

2 g carbohydrate

0 g fat

0 g saturated fat

0 mg cholesterol

60 mg sodium

DIABETIC EXCHANGE:

Free exchange

Creamy Mustard Sauce

YIELD:
1-1/4 cups
(20 servings)

PER SERVING (1 TABLESPOON):

10 calories

<1 g protein

1 g carbohydrate

<1 g fat

<1 g saturated fat

<1 mg cholesterol

45 mg sodium

DIABETIC EXCHANGE:

Free exchange

BB

1 CUP BASIC WHITE SAUCE (PAGE 90)

2 TABLESPOONS MINCED FRESH ONION

2 TABLESPOONS LIQUEFIED BUTTER BUDS MIX

1/2 CUP WHITE WINE OR REDUCED-SODIUM CHICKEN BROTH

1-1/2 TABLESPOONS DIJON-STYLE MUSTARD

1 TABLESPOON MINCED FRESH PARSLEY

BLACK PEPPER, TO TASTE

Prepare the Basic White Sauce; keep warm. In a small saucepan over medium heat, cook the onion in the Butter Buds until softened. Add the wine and cook until reduced to 2 tablespoons. Whisk the mixture into the sauce with the mustard, parsley, and pepper until well blended. Stir over low heat until warmed through. Serve over fish, chicken, steak, or vegetables.

Curry Sauce

1 CUP BASIC WHITE SAUCE (PAGE 90)
2 TABLESPOONS MINCED FRESH ONION
1-1/2 TEASPOONS CURRY POWDER, OR TO TASTE
2 TABLESPOONS LIQUEFIED BUTTER BUDS MIX
1/2 CUP WHITE WINE OR REDUCED-SODIUM CHICKEN BROTH

Prepare the Basic White Sauce; keep warm. In a small saucepan over medium heat, cook the onion and curry in the Butter Buds until the onion is softened. Add the wine and cook until reduced to 2 tablespoons. Whisk the mixture into the sauce until well blended. Stir over low heat until heated through. Serve on chicken or fish, steamed vegetables, or rice.

NOTE: Additional curry powder may be used to achieve a spicier flavor, if desired.

YIELD:
1 cup (16 servings)

PER SERVING (1 TABLESPOON):

5 calories

<1 g protein

2 g carbohydrate

<1 g fat

0 g saturated fat

0 mg cholesterol

45 mg sodium

DIABETIC EXCHANGE:

Free exchange

Basic Marinara Sauce

YIELD:
2-1/4 cups
(9 servings)

PER SERVING
(1/4 CUP):

5 calories

<1 g protein

2 g carbohydrate

<1 g fat

<1 g saturated fat

0 mg cholesterol

65 mg sodium

DIABETIC
EXCHANGE:

Free exchange

2 CUPS CANNED CRUSHED TOMATOES

1/3 CUP BASIC GARLIC SAUCE (PAGE 86)

1/4 CUP WHITE ZINFANDEL WINE

1 PACKET SWEET 'N LOW

In a medium saucepan, combine all the ingredients. Bring to a boil over medium heat. Reduce the heat and simmer 20 minutes, stirring occasionally. The sauce will keep, covered, in the refrigerator several days, or it may be frozen in airtight containers.

TIP: A 28-ounce can of crushed tomatoes yields 3 cups. Freeze the remaining cup of tomatoes for use in Chicken Cacciatore (page 99), if desired.

Honey-Mustard Dip

1 CUP YOGURT CHEESE (PAGE 53)

1 TABLESPOON DIJON-STYLE MUSTARD

1 TABLESPOON HONEY

3 PACKETS (OR 1 TEASPOON BULK) SWEET 'N LOW

In a small bowl, combine all the ingredients; stir until well blended. Cover and refrigerate until ready to use. The dip will keep in the refrigerator up to 1 week. If a thinner consistency is desired, for use as a sauce for cooked chicken or seafood, or as a salad dressing, simply stir in a few tablespoons of reduced-sodium chicken broth or low-fat milk.

YIELD:
1 cup
(16 servings)

PER SERVING (1 TABLESPOON):

10 calories

<1 g protein

2 g carbohydrate

0 g fat

0 g saturated fat

<1 mg cholesterol

30 mg sodium

DIABETIC EXCHANGE:

Free exchange

Horseradish Dip

YIELD:
1 cup (8 servings)

PER SERVING
(2
TABLESPOONS):

35 calories

3 g protein

5 g carbohydrate

0 g fat

0 g saturated fat

<1 mg cholesterol

69 mg sodium

DIABETIC
EXCHANGE:

1/2 nonfat milk
exchange

1 CUP YOGURT CHEESE (PAGE 53)

1/4 CUP FINELY CHOPPED ONION

3 TO 4 TEASPOONS PREPARED HORSERADISH

2 PACKETS SWEET 'N LOW

In a small bowl, combine all the ingredients; stir until well blended. Cover and refrigerate until ready to use. The dip will keep in the refrigerator for up to 1 week. Serve with Chicken Fingers (page 47) or as a dip for raw vegetables.

NOTE: If a thinner consistency is desired, for use as a sauce for cooked meat, chicken, or seafood, simply stir in a few tablespoons of reduced-sodium chicken broth or low-fat milk.

TIP: For a colorful presentation, halve sweet yellow and red peppers lengthwise, remove the seeds and membrane, and fill with Horesradish Dip.

The Main Event

Saffron Scallops with Angel Hair Pasta,

Rosemary Roasted Chicken Breasts, Beef

Stir-Fry—our entrées look great, taste great, *are*

great! We've kept the calories, fat, and sodium

low, while adding blends of herbs and spices

for extraordinary flavor.

Rosemary Roasted Chicken Breasts

YIELD:
6 chicken breast
halves (12 servings)

**PER SERVING
(1 CHICKEN
BREAST HALF):**

150 calories

26 g protein

1 g carbohydrate

4 g fat

1 g saturated fat

70 mg cholesterol

70 mg sodium

**DIABETIC
EXCHANGE:**

3 lean meat
exchanges

1/4 CUP LIQUEFIED BUTTER BUDS MIX

1/4 CUP DRY WHITE WINE OR REDUCED-SODIUM CHICKEN BROTH

1 TABLESPOON LEMON JUICE

1 TABLESPOON CHOPPED FRESH ROSEMARY

1 TEASPOON SALT-FREE GARLIC-AND-HERB SEASONING BLEND

6 CHICKEN BREAST HALVES, SKINNED (4 OUNCES EACH)

Preheat the oven to 425°F.

In a small bowl, combine all the ingredients, except the chicken. Place the chicken in a roasting pan; brush both sides with the Butter Buds mixture. Roast 45 minutes, or until cooked through, basting with any remaining mixture.

NOTE: Reserve 2 cooked chicken breast halves for Chicken Fajitas (page 54), if desired.

TIP: When using fresh herbs, use 3 times the amount suggested for dried herbs.

Chicken Cacciatore

6 SKINLESS CHICKEN BREAST HALVES, CUT INTO PIECES (APPROXIMATELY 2-1/2 POUNDS)

1 LARGE GREEN BELL PEPPER, CUT INTO CHUNKS

1 MEDIUM ONION, SLICED

1 CUP CANNED CRUSHED TOMATOES

1/2 CUP REDUCED-SODIUM CHICKEN BROTH OR DRY WHITE WINE

1/2 TEASPOON DRIED THYME LEAVES, CRUMBLED

1/8 TEASPOON EACH: SALT AND PEPPER

1/3 CUP BASIC GARLIC SAUCE (PAGE 86)

2 TEASPOONS BUTTER BUDS MIX, DRY (OR 1-1/2 TEASPOONS BUTTER BUDS SPRINKLES)

2 CUPS COOKED RICE OR PASTA, WITHOUT ADDED FAT OR SALT

FRESH PARSLEY SPRIGS, FOR GARNISH

Spray a large nonstick skillet with nonstick cooking spray and heat over medium-high heat. When hot, add the chicken pieces. Brown well on all sides. Add the bell pepper and onion; cook 2 minutes. In a 2-cup measure, stir the tomatoes, broth, and seasonings into the Basic Garlic Sauce. Add to the skillet and bring to a boil. Reduce the heat, cover, and simmer 20 to 30 minutes, or until the chicken is cooked through. Stir the Butter Buds into the rice or pasta and spoon onto a serving platter. Spoon the chicken mixture over the rice or pasta. Garnish with parsley sprigs.

NOTE: Additional vegetables, such as fresh mushrooms and sliced fresh zucchini, may be added with the bell pepper and onions, if desired.

YIELD:
6 servings

PER SERVING:
255 calories
29 g protein
25 g carbohydrate
3 g fat
1 g saturated fat
75 mg cholesterol
160 mg sodium

DIABETIC EXCHANGES:
1 starch/bread exchange
1 vegetable exchange
3 lean meat exchanges

Sweet-and-Sour Chicken

YIELD:
approximately 5-1/3
cups (4 servings)

**PER SERVING
(1-1/3 CUPS):**

350 calories

21 g protein

50 g carbohydrate

7 g fat

2 g saturated fat

70 mg cholesterol

160 mg sodium

**DIABETIC
EXCHANGES:**

2 starch/bread
exchanges

1 fruit exchange

1 vegetable
exchange

2 lean meat
exchanges

**1 CAN (8 OUNCES) PINEAPPLE CHUNKS PACKED IN
UNSWEETENED JUICE**

12 OUNCES SKINLESS, BONELESS CHICKEN BREASTS, CUBED

**1 MEDIUM BELL PEPPER (GREEN, RED, OR YELLOW),
CUT INTO CHUNKS (1 CUP)**

1 SMALL ONION, CUT INTO CHUNKS (1/2 CUP)

1/8 TEASPOON EACH: SALT AND PEPPER

2 CUPS SNOW PEAS (ABOUT 8 OUNCES)

3/4 CUP SWEET-AND-SOUR SAUCE (PAGE 82)

1 TEASPOON BUTTER BUDS SPRINKLES

2 CUPS COOKED RICE, WITHOUT ADDED FAT OR SALT

Drain the pineapple, reserving the juice. Spray a large nonstick skillet with
nonstick cooking spray and heat over high heat. When hot, add the chicken,
bell pepper, onion, salt, and pepper. Cook, stirring constantly, 3 to 4 minutes,
or until the chicken is lightly browned. Add the reserved pineapple juice and
snow peas. Reduce the heat to medium-low, cover, and cook 3 to 5 minutes,
or until the chicken is cooked through. Stir in the Sweet-and-Sour Sauce
and pineapple; cook until heated through. Season with additional pepper, if
desired. Stir the Butter Buds into the cooked rice and place on a serving
plate. Spoon the chicken mixture over the rice.

Turkey Chili

1 POUND LEAN GROUND TURKEY

1 TABLESPOON BUTTER BUDS SPRINKLES

2 TEASPOONS CHILI POWDER

1 TEASPOON DRIED OREGANO, CRUMBLED

3 CUPS UNCOOKED GARDEN FRESH SALSA (PAGE 51)

1/3 CUP NO-SALT-ADDED TOMATO PASTE

1 BAY LEAF

FRESHLY GROUND BLACK PEPPER, TO TASTE

2 CUPS COOKED RICE, OPTIONAL

Spray a large nonstick skillet with nonstick cooking spray and heat over medium-high heat. When hot, add the turkey; brown. Stir in the Butter Buds, chili powder, and oregano; cook 1 minute. Stir in the salsa, tomato paste, bay leaf, and pepper. Reduce the heat, cover, and simmer 30 minutes. Serve over cooked rice, if desired.

YIELD:
4 cups (4 servings)

PER SERVING (1 CUP):

210 calories

30 g protein

11 g carbohydrate

4 g fat

1 g saturated fat

70 mg cholesterol

145 mg sodium

DIABETIC EXCHANGES:

2 vegetable exchanges

3 lean meat exchanges

YIELD:
7-1/2 cups (5 servings)

PER SERVING (1-1/2 CUPS):

210 calories

28 g protein

17 g carbohydrate

3 g fat

1 g saturated fat

55 mg cholesterol

290 mg sodium

DIABETIC EXCHANGES:

1/2 starch/bread exchange

2 vegetable exchanges

3 lean meat exchanges

𝓑𝓑

Chili with Beans

Prepare the recipe as directed above without rice; stir in *1 can (15-1/2 to 16 ounces) drained and rinsed kidney beans.* Cook until heated through.

Turkey-Couscous Pita Pockets

2 CUPS COUSCOUS SALAD (PAGE 71)
6 OUNCES (1-1/2 CUPS) DICED COOKED TURKEY
6 WHOLE WHEAT MINI PITA BREADS
ALFALFA SPROUTS, FOR GARNISH

In a medium bowl, combine the Couscous Salad and turkey. Cut a thin slice from each pita to form a pocket. Fill each pita pocket with 1/2 cup salad; garnish with alfalfa sprouts.

YIELD:
6 pitas (6 servings)

**PER SERVING
(1 PITA):**

185 calories

10 g protein

26 g carbohydrate

3 g fat

1 g saturated fat

25 mg cholesterol

470 mg sodium

**DIABETIC
EXCHANGES:**

1-1/2 starch/bread
exchanges

1 lean meat
exchange

Turkey Skillet Dinner

YIELD:
6 cups (4 servings)

**PER SERVING
(1-1/2 CUPS):**

300 calories

30 g protein

35 g carbohydrate

3 g fat

1 g saturated fat

60 mg cholesterol

215 mg sodium

**DIABETIC
EXCHANGES:**

2 starch/bread
exchanges

1 vegetable
exchange

3 lean meat
exchanges

1 LARGE ONION, DICED

1 LARGE GARLIC CLOVE, MINCED

12 OUNCES COOKED TURKEY BREAST, DICED

1 CAN (14-1/2 OUNCES) NO-SALT-ADDED STEWED TOMATOES

1 CAN (10-1/2 OUNCES) REDUCED-SODIUM CHICKEN BROTH

2 CUPS FROZEN DICED MIXED VEGETABLES FOR SOUP

3/4 CUP UNCOOKED INSTANT RICE

1 TABLESPOON BUTTER BUDS SPRINKLES

2 TABLESPOONS NO-SALT-ADDED TOMATO PASTE

1 TEASPOON SALT-FREE GARLIC-AND-HERB SEASONING BLEND

1/8 TEASPOON SALT

FRESHLY GROUND BLACK PEPPER, TO TASTE

Spray a large nonstick skillet with nonstick cooking spray and heat over medium heat. When hot, add the onion and garlic; cook 3 minutes. Stir in the turkey; cook 1 minute. Add the remaining ingredients to the skillet and stir until well blended. Bring the mixture to a boil; reduce the heat, cover, and simmer 25 minutes, or until the vegetables are tender and most of the liquid has been absorbed.

Honey-Citrus Glazed Turkey Breast

ONE 5- TO 5-1/2-POUND WHOLE TURKEY BREAST, THAWED

1 PACKET BUTTER BUDS MIX, DRY

1/4 CUP HOT WATER

2 TABLESPOONS EACH: HONEY, LEMON JUICE, LIME JUICE

1-1/2 TEASPOONS SALT-FREE ALL-PURPOSE SEASONING BLEND

Preheat the oven to 325°F.

Rinse the turkey breast and pat dry. Using a small sharp knife and your hands, loosen the skin all around the breast, but leave intact at the sides. In a small bowl, combine the Butter Buds and water; stir in honey, lemon juice, and lime juice. Lift the skin of the turkey breast and brush the entire surface with some of the glaze. Place skin-side down in the roasting pan. Brush the entire cavity with some of the glaze; sprinkle the cavity with some of the seasoning blend. Roast 1 hour, basting occasionally. Turn the breast skin-side up; brush with the glaze and sprinkle with the remaining seasoning blend. Continue roasting 1 to 1-1/2 hours, basting with the remaining glaze until the turkey is done. Cool about 20 minutes before slicing. Remove the skin before serving, if desired.

TIP: To make your own reduced-sodium turkey broth, simmer the left-over turkey rib cage in water to cover with diced carrot, onion, celery, and fresh parsley sprigs for approximately 90 minutes.

YIELD:
Approximately 13 servings

PER SERVING (3 OUNCES):

150 calories

27 g protein

3 g carbohydrate

3 g fat

1 g saturated fat

60 mg cholesterol

100 mg sodium

DIABETIC EXCHANGES:

3 lean meat exchanges

Fish Fillets with Asparagus

YIELD:
4 servings

**PER SERVING
(1 FILLET WITH
ASPARAGUS):**

135 calories

24 g protein

4 g carbohydrate

2 g fat

<1 g saturated fat

65 mg cholesterol

145 mg sodium

**DIABETIC
EXCHANGES:**

1 vegetable
exchange

3 lean meat
exchanges

8 OUNCES FRESH ASPARAGUS SPEARS

1/2 CUP DRY WHITE WINE OR REDUCED-SODIUM CHICKEN BROTH

1/4 CUP WATER

2 TABLESPOONS MINCED SHALLOTS

1 GARLIC CLOVE, MINCED

2 TEASPOONS BUTTER BUDS SPRINKLES

1 TEASPOON SALT-FREE LEMON-AND-PEPPER SEASONING

4 FRESH FLOUNDER OR SOLE FILLETS (4 OUNCES EACH)

1/4 CUP LOW-FAT MILK

1 TEASPOON CORNSTARCH

Trim the asparagus spears and cut in half crosswise. In a large skillet, combine the wine, water, shallots, garlic, Butter Buds, and seasoning. Bring to a boil over medium-high heat; add the asparagus. Reduce the heat, cover, and simmer 4 to 5 minutes, or until the asparagus are almost tender. Remove from the heat and cool slightly. Remove the asparagus with a slotted spoon.

Place the fish fillets on a flat surface, arrange an equal amount of asparagus on each fillet, roll up fillets, and return to skillet, seam-side down. Cook over medium-low heat, covered, 10 minutes, or until the fish is opaque. Transfer the fillets to a serving platter; cover and keep warm. Combine the milk and cornstarch; stir into the skillet. Increase the heat to medium and cook, stirring constantly, 1 to 2 minutes, or until the mixture thickens and comes to a boil. Spoon over the fillets.

Phyllo-Baked Fish with Creamy Sauce

YIELD:
4 servings

PER SERVING:

195 calories

26 g protein

17 g carbohydrate

2 g fat

<1 g saturated fat

65 mg cholesterol

215 mg sodium

DIABETIC EXCHANGES:

1 starch/bread exchange

1 vegetable exchange

3 lean meat exchanges

8 OUNCES FRESH ASPARAGUS SPEARS

1/2 CUP DRY WHITE WINE OR REDUCED-SODIUM CHICKEN BROTH

1/4 CUP WATER

2 TABLESPOONS MINCED SHALLOTS

1 GARLIC CLOVE, MINCED

2 TEASPOONS BUTTER BUDS SPRINKLES

1 TEASPOON SALT-FREE LEMON-AND-PEPPER SEASONING

4 FRESH FLOUNDER OR SOLE FILLETS (4 OUNCES EACH)

4 SHEETS PHYLLO DOUGH

1/4 CUP LOWFAT MILK

1 TEASPOON CORNSTARCH

Trim the asparagus spears and cut in half crosswise. In a large skillet, combine the wine, water, shallots, garlic, Butter Buds, and seasoning. Bring to a boil over medium-high heat; add the asparagus. Reduce the heat, cover, and simmer 4 to 5 minutes, or until the asparagus are almost tender. Remove from the heat and cool slightly. Remove the asparagus with a slotted spoon.

Preheat the oven to 350°F.

Place the fish fillets on a flat surface, arrange an equal amount of asparagus on each fillet, and roll up fillets. On a flat surface, spray one sheet phyllo dough with nonstick cooking spray. Place one rolled fillet, seam-side down, at the narrow end of the phyllo dough. Fold the sides over to cover the fillet. Roll up and place on a baking sheet. Spray the surface with nonstick cooking spray. Repeat with the remaining phyllo dough and fillets. Bake 20 minutes. Turn the wrapped fillet over and pierce with a fork. If the fish is flaky and opaque, it is done. Meanwhile, heat the pan juices over medium heat. In a small bowl, combine the milk and cornstarch. Stir into the skillet. Cook, stirring constantly, 1 to 2 minutes, or until the mixture thickens and comes to a boil. Transfer the fillets to a serving platter and spoon sauce over the fillets.

YIELD:
6 cakes
(6 servings)

**PER SERVING
(1 CAKE):**

130 calories

12 g protein

6 g carbohydrate

5 g fat

1 g saturated fat

16 mg cholesterol

125 mg sodium

**DIABETIC
EXCHANGES:**

1/2 starch/bread
exchange

1-1/2 lean meat
exchanges

Salmon-Dill Cakes

1 CAN (15-1/2 OUNCES) SALMON, DRAINED AND RINSED

3/4 CUP FINELY SHREDDED ZUCCHINI

1/4 CUP PLAIN DRY BREAD CRUMBS

2 TABLESPOONS REDUCED-CALORIE MAYONNAISE

2 TABLESPOONS MINCED DRIED ONION

1 TABLESPOON BUTTER BUDS SPRINKLES

1 TABLESPOON LEMON JUICE

1 TABLESPOON PARSLEY FLAKES

1 TEASPOON DILL WEED

1 LARGE EGG WHITE

In a medium bowl, mash the salmon. Stir in the next 8 ingredients. Add the egg white, stirring until well blended. Spray a large nonstick skillet with nonstick cooking spray and heat over medium heat. Shape the salmon mixture into 6 patties. Add to the skillet and cook 3 to 4 minutes on each side, or until golden.

TIP: Salmon is high in omega-3 fatty acids, which are thought to help promote heart health.

Saffron Scallops with Angel Hair Pasta

YIELD:
7 cups (4 servings)

PER SERVING (1-3/4 CUPS):

355 calories

27 g protein

50 g carbohydrate

7 g fat

1 g saturated fat

40 mg cholesterol

420 mg sodium

DIABETIC EXCHANGES:

3 starch/bread exchanges

2 lean meat exchanges

1/4 CUP LIQUEFIED BUTTER BUDS MIX, DIVIDED

1 TABLESPOON MARGARINE

1/4 CUP MINCED SHALLOTS

1 SMALL GARLIC CLOVE, MINCED

3 TABLESPOONS ALL-PURPOSE FLOUR

1/2 CUP REDUCED-SODIUM CHICKEN BROTH

1/2 CUP DRY WHITE WINE

1/2 TEASPOON SAFFRON THREADS

1/2 TEASPOON DRIED THYME LEAVES, CRUMBLED

1/2 CUP LOW-FAT MILK

2 TABLESPOONS LIGHT CREAM OR HALF-AND-HALF

1 POUND BAY SCALLOPS (OR SEA SCALLOPS, QUARTERED)

1 SMALL ZUCCHINI, JULIENNE-CUT (1 CUP)

1 MEDIUM TOMATO, PEELED, SEEDED, AND CHOPPED (3/4 CUP)

1 TABLESPOON FRESH LEMON JUICE

1/2 TEASPOON DRIED MARJORAM, CRUMBLED

1/8 TEASPOON RED PEPPER FLAKES

FRESHLY GROUND BLACK PEPPER, TO TASTE

1 PACKAGE (9 OUNCES) FRESH ANGEL HAIR PASTA

In a large skillet over medium heat, combine 2 tablespoons Butter Buds and margarine; add the shallots and garlic and cook 3 minutes, stirring constantly. Add the flour and cook, stirring constantly, 2 to 3 minutes. In a 1-cup measure, combine the broth, wine, saffron, and thyme. Gradually add to the skillet, stirring constantly to make a smooth sauce. Cook and stir until thickened and smooth. Stir in the milk, cream, and remaining Butter Buds. Cook an additional 2 minutes. Reduce the heat to low. Add the scallops, zucchini, tomato, lemon juice, marjoram, and red and black pepper to the sauce. Cook, covered, 7 to 10 minutes, or until the scallops are opaque. Cook the pasta according to package directions but without salt. Drain and place on a large serving platter. Spoon the scallop mixture over the pasta; toss lightly.

Linguine with Herbed Clam Sauce

2 CANS (6-1/2 OUNCES EACH) CHOPPED CLAMS

1 CAN (10 OUNCES) ALL-NATURAL CLAM JUICE

1 PACKET BUTTER BUDS MIX, DRY (OR 2 TABLESPOONS
BUTTER BUDS SPRINKLES)

2 TABLESPOONS MINCED FRESH PARSLEY

2 LARGE GARLIC CLOVES, MINCED

1 TEASPOON DRIED OREGANO LEAVES, CRUMBLED

1 PACKAGE (9 OUNCES) FRESH LINGUINE

ADDITIONAL MINCED FRESH PARSLEY, FOR GARNISH

FAT-FREE PARMESAN CHEESE TOPPING, OPTIONAL

YIELD:
6 cups (4 servings)

**PER SERVING
(1-1/2 CUPS):**

240 calories

15 g protein

42 g carbohydrate

3 g fat

<1 g saturated fat

55 mg cholesterol

440 mg sodium

**DIABETIC
EXCHANGES:**

2-1/2 starch/bread
exchanges

1 lean meat
exchange

Drain the clams, reserving the juice. In a medium saucepan, combine all the clam juices, Butter Buds, parsley, garlic, and oregano. Bring to a boil over medium heat. Reduce the heat and simmer 10 minutes. Stir in the chopped clams. Cook the pasta according to package directions but without salt. Drain and place on a large serving platter. Spoon the sauce over the linguine and toss to coat. Sprinkle with additional parsley and serve with Parmesan cheese topping, if desired.

TIP: Most pasta approximately doubles in bulk when cooked.

Penne with Broccoli and Garlic

YIELD:
6 cups (4 servings)

**PER SERVING
(1-1/2 CUPS):**

310 calories

16 g protein

50 g carbohydrate

6 g fat

1 g saturated fat

5 mg cholesterol

365 mg sodium

**DIABETIC
EXCHANGES:**

2-1/2 starch/bread
exchanges

2 vegetable
exchanges

1/2 lean meat
exchange

1 fat exchange

8 OUNCES UNCOOKED PENNE OR ZITI MACARONI

1 TABLESPOON OLIVE OIL

2 HEADS FRESH BROCCOLI, TRIMMED AND CUT INTO BITE-SIZE
PIECES (ABOUT 1-1/2 POUNDS)

1 TABLESPOON MINCED FRESH GARLIC

2 OUNCES CANADIAN BACON, CUT INTO THIN STRIPS

1/2 CUP DRY WHITE WINE

1/4 CUP REDUCED-SODIUM CHICKEN BROTH

2 TABLESPOONS BUTTER BUDS SPRINKLES

2 TEASPOONS SALT-FREE GARLIC-AND-HERB SEASONING BLEND

1/2 TEASPOON DRIED THYME LEAVES, CRUMBLED

1/8 TEASPOON SALT

FRESHLY GROUND BLACK PEPPER, TO TASTE

FAT-FREE GRATED PARMESAN ITALIAN TOPPING, OPTIONAL

Cook the penne or ziti macaroni according to package directions but without salt. In a large nonstick skillet over medium-high heat, heat the oil. When hot, add the broccoli, garlic, and bacon. Cook, stirring constantly, for 5 minutes. Add the wine, broth, Butter Buds, and seasonings to the skillet; bring to a boil. Reduce the heat, cover, and simmer 5 to 7 minutes, or until the broccoli is crisp-tender. Drain the pasta and stir into the broccoli mixture. Sprinkle with Parmesan topping, if desired.

TIP: Broccoli—along with brussels sprouts, cabbage, cauliflower, kale, and mustard greens—is a cruciferous vegetable. Cruciferous vegetables may be protective against certain cancers.

Beef Stir-Fry

12 OUNCES BEEF ROUND STEAK

2 TABLESPOONS DRY SHERRY

1 TABLESPOON REDUCED-SODIUM SOY SAUCE

1 TEASPOON EACH: MINCED FRESH GARLIC AND
MINCED FRESH GINGER

1 PACKET SWEET 'N LOW

1 LARGE ONION, CUT INTO WEDGES

1 LARGE RED BELL PEPPER, CUT INTO CHUNKS

6 OUNCES FRESH SNOW PEAS

3/4 CUP REDUCED-SODIUM BEEF BROTH

1 TABLESPOON CORNSTARCH DISSOLVED IN 2 TABLESPOONS
COLD WATER

2 CUPS COOKED RICE, WITHOUT ADDED FAT OR SALT

2 TEASPOONS BUTTER BUDS SPRINKLES

YIELD:
4 cups (4 servings)

**PER SERVING
(1 CUP):**

355 calories

24 g protein

42 g carbohydrate

9 g fat

4 g saturated fat

50 mg cholesterol

245 mg sodium

**DIABETIC
EXCHANGES:**

2-1/2 starch/bread
exchanges

1 vegetable
exchange

2 lean meat
exchanges

Partially freeze the beef to make cutting easier, if desired. Slice on the diagonal into very thin strips.

In a shallow dish, combine the sherry, soy sauce, garlic, ginger, and Sweet 'N Low. Add the beef and toss to coat. Cover and refrigerate 1 hour. Heat a large nonstick skillet over high heat. Add the onion and pepper; cook, stirring constantly, for 3 minutes. Transfer to a bowl and set aside. Return the skillet to the heat. Add the beef with the marinade; cook, stirring constantly, for 3 minutes, or until the beef is almost cooked through. Return the onion and pepper to the skillet with the snow peas and broth. Bring to a boil; reduce the heat, cover, and simmer 5 minutes. Stir in the cornstarch mixture and cook until thickened and bubbly. Combine the rice and Butter Buds; spoon onto a serving platter. Top with the beef-vegetable mixture.

TIP: Most rice approximately triples in bulk after cooking. Therefore you need 1/3 cup uncooked rice for each cup cooked rice desired.

The Grand Finale

Sinfully scrumptious Brownie Sundae Pie,
delicate Almond Cookies, delectable Cherry
Crisp, fluffy Banana Cream Pie—these desserts
are enough to make any occasion special.
Healthy eating never tasted so sweet!

YIELD:
3 dozen cookies
(18 servings)

**PER SERVING
(2 COOKIES):**

95 calories

2 g protein

15 g carbohydrate

3 g fat

1 g saturated fat

0 mg cholesterol

85 mg sodium

**DIABETIC
EXCHANGES:**

1 starch/bread
exchange

1/2 fat exchange

Oatmeal Raisin Cookies

1-1/2 CUPS QUICK-COOKING OATS

3/4 CUP ALL-PURPOSE FLOUR

1/2 TEASPOON GROUND CINNAMON

1/2 TEASPOON BAKING POWDER

1/4 TEASPOON GROUND GINGER

1/8 TEASPOON SALT

1/2 CUP REDUCED-CALORIE STICK MARGARINE

1/3 CUP LIGHT BROWN SUGAR, PACKED TO MEASURE

4 PACKETS (OR 1-1/4 TEASPOONS BULK) SWEET 'N LOW

2 EGG WHITES

1 TEASPOON VANILLA EXTRACT

1/3 CUP RAISINS

Preheat the oven to 375°F.

In a medium bowl, combine the oats, flour, cinnamon, baking powder, ginger, and salt; set aside. In a large bowl, mix the margarine, sugar, Sweet 'N Low, egg whites, and vanilla with an electric beater. Stir in the dry ingredients until well blended. Add the raisins. Spray cookie sheets with nonstick cooking spray. Drop the dough by rounded teaspoonfuls onto cookie sheets. Bake 8 to 10 minutes, or until lightly browned. Cool on a wire rack.

TIP: Dark metal or dark-colored nonstick baking sheets produce browner cookies than shiny metal or light-colored nonstick baking sheets.

Oatmeal Chocolate Chip Cookies

Prepare the cookie dough as directed for Oatmeal Raisin Cookies except: *Omit the cinnamon and ginger*, increase *the vanilla extract to 1-1/2 teaspoons*, and use *1/3 cup mini semisweet chocolate chips instead of raisins*.

YIELD:

3 dozen cookies
(18 servings)

**PER SERVING
(2 COOKIES):**

100 calories

2 g protein

15 g carbohydrate

4 g fat

1 g saturated fat

0 mg cholesterol

85 mg sodium

**DIABETIC
EXCHANGES:**

1 starch/bread
exchange

1 fat exchange

YIELD:
2-1/2 dozen cookies
(15 servings)

**PER SERVING
(2 COOKIES):**

80 calories

2 g protein

14 g carbohydrate

2 g fat

<1 g saturated fat

10 mg cholesterol

80 mg sodium

**DIABETIC
EXCHANGE:**

1 starch/bread
exchange

Almond Cookies

1 CUP PLUS 2 TABLESPOONS ALL-PURPOSE FLOUR

1/2 CUP SUGAR

2 TABLESPOONS BUTTER BUDS SPRINKLES

1/2 TEASPOON BAKING POWDER

1/8 TEASPOON SALT

4 TABLESPOONS REDUCED-CALORIE STICK MARGARINE

1 LARGE EGG

2 TEASPOONS ALMOND EXTRACT

1 TABLESPOON SLICED ALMONDS

In a medium bowl, combine the flour, sugar, Butter Buds, baking powder, and salt. With a pastry blender or 2 knives used scissor fashion, cut in the margarine until the mixture resembles coarse crumbs. Stir in the egg and almond extract to make a soft dough. Cover and refrigerate 1 hour, or until well chilled.

Preheat the oven to 350°F.

Spray cookie sheets with nonstick cooking spray. Shape dough into 1-inch balls and place on cookie sheets. Press 1 almond slice in the center of each ball. Bake 12 to 15 minutes, or until golden brown. Remove to wire rack to cool.

TIP: To retain freshness, store cooled cookies in plastic bags or tightly covered containers. Coffee cans with plastic lids make good substitute cookie jars.

Creamy Rice Pudding

2-3/4 CUPS 1% FAT MILK, DIVIDED

1 PACKET BUTTER BUDS MIX, LIQUEFIED

1/2 CUP EVAPORATED SKIM MILK

1/2 CUP UNCOOKED LONG-GRAIN RICE

1/4 CUP SUGAR

3 TABLESPOONS CORNSTARCH

1 LARGE EGG YOLK

1/4 CUP RAISINS

3 PACKETS (OR 1 TEASPOON BULK) SWEET 'N LOW

1 TEASPOON VANILLA EXTRACT

1/2 TEASPOON GROUND CINNAMON, PLUS ADDITIONAL CINNAMON FOR SPRINKLING

In a large saucepan, combine 2 cups 1% fat milk, Butter Buds, evaporated skim milk, rice, and sugar. Bring to a boil over medium heat. Reduce the heat, cover, and simmer 30 minutes, stirring occasionally. Stir the cornstarch into the remaining 3/4 cup 1% fat milk. Add to the rice mixture. Cook, stirring constantly, until thickened. In a small bowl, beat the egg yolk. Stir in 1/2 cup hot rice mixture, then add back into the saucepan. Cook, stirring constantly, for 1 minute. Add the raisins, Sweet 'N Low, vanilla, and cinnamon. Stir until well blended. Pour the pudding into a 1-quart dish. Sprinkle with additional cinnamon and cool to room temperature. Serve at room temperature, if desired, or refrigerate until served.

YIELD:
4 cups (8 servings)

PER SERVING (1/2 CUP):

155 calories

5 g protein

30 g carbohydrate

2 g fat

1 g saturated fat

30 mg cholesterol

135 mg sodium

DIABETIC EXCHANGES:

1/2 low-fat milk exchange

1 starch/bread exchange

1/2 fruit exchange

YIELD:
2 cups (4 servings)

PER SERVING (1/2 CUP):

180 calories

6 g protein

30 g carbohydrate

4 g fat

1 g saturated fat

60 mg cholesterol

85 mg sodium

DIABETIC EXCHANGES:

1/2 low-fat milk exchange

1-1/2 starch/bread exchanges

Delectable Chocolate Pudding

2 CUPS 1% FAT MILK

1/4 CUP CORNSTARCH

1/4 CUP SUGAR

3 PACKETS (OR 1 TEASPOON BULK) SWEET 'N LOW

2 TABLESPOONS EUROPEAN-STYLE UNSWEETENED COCOA POWDER

2 TEASPOONS BUTTER BUDS MIX, DRY (OR 1-1/2 TEASPOONS BUTTER BUDS SPRINKLES)

1 LARGE EGG YOLK

1 TEASPOON VANILLA EXTRACT

In the top of a double boiler, combine the milk and cornstarch; stir to dissolve the cornstarch. Add the sugar, Sweet 'N Low, cocoa, and Butter Buds. Over boiling water, cook, stirring constantly, for 12 to 15 minutes, until the mixture is thickened and smooth. In a small bowl, beat the egg yolk; gradually add about 1/2 cup pudding mixture, stirring constantly. Add the egg mixture back into the pudding; cook, stirring constantly, about 2 minutes, until thickened and smooth. Remove from the heat and stir in the vanilla. Transfer the pudding to a bowl; cover the surface with plastic wrap. Refrigerate several hours until cold.

Creamy Chocolate Pudding

1 CUP REDUCED-CALORIE FROZEN WHIPPED TOPPING

2 CUPS DELECTABLE CHOCOLATE PUDDING (PAGE 120)

In a medium bowl, fold the whipped topping into the chocolate pudding until well blended. Pour into 6 individual serving dishes. Refrigerate until ready to serve.

NOTE: The pudding may be poured into a Graham Cracker Crust (page 122).

YIELD:
3 cups (6 servings)

PER SERVING (1/2 CUP):

143 calories

4 g protein

23 g carbohydrate

4 g fat

1 g saturated fat

39 mg cholesterol

57 mg sodium

DIABETIC EXCHANGES:

1/2 low-fat milk exchange

1 starch/bread exchange

YIELD:
1 nine-inch piecrust
(8 servings)

PER SERVING:

75 calories

1 g protein

12 g carbohydrate

2 g fat

<1 g saturated fat

0 mg cholesterol

100 mg sodium

**DIABETIC
EXCHANGE:**

1 starch/bread
exchange

Graham Cracker Crust

16 GRAHAM CRACKER SQUARES, CRUSHED

1 TABLESPOON SUGAR

1 TEASPOON GROUND CINNAMON

1-1/2 TABLESPOONS LIQUEFIED BUTTER BUDS MIX

1 TABLESPOON MARGARINE, MELTED

Preheat the oven to 350°F.

In a small bowl, stir together the first 3 ingredients. Add the Butter Buds and margarine; stir until blended. Press into the bottom and up the sides of a 9-inch pie plate. Bake 8 minutes. Cool on a wire rack.

TIP: For an easy dessert, fill a low-fat Graham Cracker Crust with low-fat pudding, frozen yogurt, whipped topping, or canned fruit.

Harvest Pumpkin Squares

3/4 CUP ALL-PURPOSE FLOUR

1/4 CUP WHEAT GERM

1/2 TEASPOON BAKING POWDER

1/2 TEASPOON GROUND CINNAMON

1/4 TEASPOON EACH: GROUND GINGER, GROUND NUTMEG,
BAKING SODA, AND SALT

1/4 CUP REDUCED-CALORIE MARGARINE

2 TABLESPOONS BUTTER BUDS SPRINKLES

2/3 CUP LIGHT BROWN SUGAR, PACKED TO MEASURE

2/3 CUP CANNED SOLID-PACK PUMPKIN

1/2 CUP LIQUID EGG SUBSTITUTE

1/2 TEASPOON VANILLA EXTRACT

1/3 CUP DRIED CURRANTS OR RAISINS

HONEY YOGURT CREAM, OPTIONAL (PAGE 137)

Preheat the oven to 350°F. Spray an 8-inch square baking pan with nonstick cooking spray.

In a medium bowl, combine the flour, wheat germ, baking powder, cinnamon, ginger, nutmeg, baking soda, and salt. In a large bowl, beat the margarine, Butter Buds, and brown sugar with an electric beater. Beat in the pumpkin, egg substitute, and vanilla. Stir in the dry ingredients until well blended; add the currants. Pour into the prepared pan. Bake 35 to 40 minutes, or until a toothpick inserted in the center comes out clean. Cool on a wire rack. Cut into 2-inch squares. Serve with Honey Yogurt Cream, flavored with 1 teaspoon grated orange peel, if desired.

TIP: Pumpkin is an excellent source of beta carotene, vitamin C, potassium, and dietary fiber. It is also low in calories. Heat canned pumpkin sprinkled with cinnamon and Sweet 'N Low in the microwave for a quick and healthy snack.

YIELD:
16 squares
(16 servings)

**PER SERVING
(1 SQUARE
WITHOUT
HONEY YOGURT
CREAM):**

100 calories

2 g protein

19 g carbohydrate

2 g fat

<1 g saturated fat

<1 mg cholesterol

125 mg sodium

**DIABETIC
EXCHANGES:**

1 starch/bread
exchange

1/2 fruit exchange

Banana Spice Cake

YIELD:
24 squares
(24 servings)

**PER SERVING
(1 SQUARE
WITHOUT
HONEY YOGURT
CREAM OR
WALNUTS):**

90 calories

2 g protein

20 g carbohydrate

<1 g fat

<1 g saturated fat

<1 mg cholesterol

85 mg sodium

**DIABETIC
EXCHANGE:**

1 starch/bread
exchange

1-1/4 CUPS SIFTED WHOLE WHEAT FLOUR

1 CUP SIFTED ALL-PURPOSE FLOUR

1 CUP SUGAR

1-1/2 TEASPOONS GROUND CINNAMON

1-1/4 TEASPOONS EACH: BAKING POWDER AND BAKING SODA

3/4 TEASPOON GROUND NUTMEG

1/2 TEASPOON GROUND CLOVES

1/8 TEASPOON SALT

1-1/4 CUPS MASHED RIPE BANANAS (ABOUT 2 MEDIUM)

2/3 CUP NO-SALT-ADDED BUTTERMILK

1 PACKET BUTTER BUDS MIX, LIQUEFIED

1/2 CUP LIQUID EGG SUBSTITUTE

2 TABLESPOONS CHOPPED WALNUTS, OPTIONAL

HONEY YOGURT CREAM, OPTIONAL, (PAGE 137)

Preheat the oven to 350°F. Spray a 13 × 9-inch baking pan with nonstick cooking spray.

In a medium bowl, combine the flours, sugar, cinnamon, baking powder, baking soda, nutmeg, cloves, and salt. In a large bowl, beat the bananas, buttermilk, Butter Buds, and egg substitute with an electric beater or a wire whisk. Add the dry ingredients until well blended. Add the walnuts, if desired. Pour into the prepared pan. Bake 25 to 30 minutes, or until a toothpick inserted in the center comes out clean. Cool on a wire rack. Cut into squares and serve with Honey Yogurt Cream, if desired.

Strawberry Shortcake

YIELD:
12 shortcakes
(12 servings)

PER SERVING
(1 SHORTCAKE
WITH BERRIES
AND WHIPPED
TOPPING):

150 calories

3 g protein

26 g carbohydrate

4 g fat

1 g saturated fat

<1 mg cholesterol

65 mg sodium

DIABETIC
EXCHANGES:

1 starch/bread
exchange

1/2 fruit exchange

1 fat exchange

Berries

1 QUART FRESH STRAWBERRIES, SLICED (ABOUT 4 CUPS)

2 TABLESPOONS SUGAR

2 PACKETS SWEET 'N LOW

In a large bowl, toss the strawberries, sugar, and Sweet 'N Low. Cover. Refrigerate until ready to serve.

Shortcakes

2 CUPS ALL-PURPOSE FLOUR

2 TABLESPOONS SUGAR

2 PACKETS SWEET 'N LOW

1 TABLESPOON BAKING POWDER

1/8 TEASPOON SALT

6 TABLESPOONS REDUCED-CALORIE STICK MARGARINE

1/3 CUP EACH: 1% FAT MILK AND REDUCED-FAT SOUR CREAM

3/4 CUP REDUCED-FAT FROZEN WHIPPED TOPPING, THAWED

Preheat the oven to 450°F. In a large bowl, combine the first 5 ingredients. With a pastry blender or 2 knives used in scissor fashion, cut in the margarine until the mixture resembles coarse crumbs. Stir in the milk and sour cream to make a soft dough. On a lightly floured surface, knead the dough 2 minutes. Press to a 3/4-inch thickness. With a 2-1/2-inch round cookie cutter, cut into 12 biscuits. Spray a cookie sheet with nonstick cooking spray. Place the biscuits on the cookie sheet 1 inch apart. Bake 10 to 12 minutes, or until the tops are golden brown. Cool on a wire rack.

To serve: Split the shortcakes in half. Spoon 1 tablespoon whipped topping onto the bottom half of each shortcake. Top with approximately 2 tablespoons sliced berries. Replace the tops. Arrange the remaining berries on top of each shortcake.

Buttermilk Cake

YIELD:
1 ten-inch cake
(10 servings)

**PER SERVING
(1/10 CAKE):**

135 calories

4 g protein

23 g carbohydrate

3 g fat

<1 g saturated fat

1 mg cholesterol

268 mg sodium

**DIABETIC
EXCHANGES:**

1-1/2 starch/bread
exchanges

1/2 fat exchange

1-1/4 CUPS CAKE FLOUR

1/2 CUP SUGAR, DIVIDED

6 PACKETS (OR 2 TEASPOONS BULK) SWEET 'N LOW

2 TEASPOONS BAKING SODA

1/8 TEASPOON SALT

3/4 CUP BUTTERMILK

2 TABLESPOONS LIQUEFIED BUTTER BUDS MIX

2 TABLESPOONS CORN OIL

1 TEASPOON VANILLA EXTRACT

6 LARGE EGG WHITES, AT ROOM TEMPERATURE

1/4 TEASPOON CREAM OF TARTAR

RASPBERRY SAUCE, OPTIONAL (PAGE 128)

STRAWBERRY SAUCE, OPTIONAL (PAGE 129)

Preheat the oven to 325°F. Spray a 10-inch round cake pan with nonstick cooking spray. Line the bottom with a circle of wax paper.

In a large bowl, combine the flour, 1/4 cup sugar, Sweet 'N Low, baking soda, and salt with an electric mixer at low speed. Continuing to mix on low speed, add the buttermilk, Butter Buds, oil, and vanilla. Mix until smooth. In a large metal bowl, beat the egg whites, remaining 1/4 cup sugar, and cream of tartar with an electric mixer at high speed until stiff but not dry. Pour the batter evenly over the egg whites; fold in gently. Pour the batter into the prepared pan. Bake 25 minutes, or until the center springs back when touched lightly. Cool on a wire rack 20 minutes. Invert onto the wire rack; remove the pan and wax paper and cool completely. Serve with fresh fruit and Raspberry or Strawberry Sauce, if desired.

Chocolate Buttermilk Cake

Reduce *the cake flour* to *1 cup.* Add *1/4 cup European-style unsweetened cocoa powder* to the dry ingredients. Proceed as directed. Dust the top with confectioners' sugar or garnish with fresh fruit, if desired.

TIP: Cake flour is made from a softer wheat than all-purpose flour. Using it in reduced-fat baked goods creates a lighter, more tender product.

YIELD:
1 ten-inch cake
(10 servings)

**PER SERVING
(1/10 CAKE):**

130 calories

4 g protein

22 g carbohydrate

3 g fat

1 g saturated fat

<1 mg cholesterol

270 mg sodium

**DIABETIC
EXCHANGES:**

1-1/2 starch/bread
exchanges

1/2 fat exchange

YIELD:
1 cup
(approximately 5
servings)

**PER SERVING
(3
TABLESPOONS):**

70 calories

<1 g protein

16 g carbohydrate

0 g fat

0 g saturated fat

0 mg cholesterol

<1 mg sodium

**DIABETIC
EXCHANGE:**

1 fruit exchange

Raspberry Sauce

**1 PACKAGE (16 OUNCES) FROZEN UNSWEETENED RASPBERRIES,
THAWED**

2 TO 3 PACKETS SWEET 'N LOW, OR TO TASTE

**1 TABLESPOON CORNSTARCH DISSOLVED IN 2 TABLESPOONS
COLD WATER**

In a food processor or blender, puree the raspberries. Strain through a colander to remove the seeds. Add the Sweet 'N Low and sweeten to taste. Stir in the cornstarch and cook 1 to 2 minutes, or until thickened and bubbly. Cool before serving. Use as a topping for crepes, fruit, or cake.

Strawberry Sauce

2 CUPS FROZEN UNSWEETENED STRAWBERRIES, THAWED

2 PACKETS SWEET 'N LOW, OR TO TASTE

1 TABLESPOON CORNSTARCH DISSOLVED IN 2 TABLESPOONS COLD WATER

Puree the strawberries and pour into a small saucepan. Add the Sweet 'N Low and cook over medium heat. Stir the cornstarch mixture into the strawberries and cook 1 to 2 minutes, or until thickened and bubbly. Cool before serving. Use as a topping for crepes, fruit, or cake.

YIELD:
1 cup
(approximately 5 servings)

PER SERVING (3 TABLESPOONS):

30 calories

<1 g protein

6 g carbohydrate

0 g fat

0 g saturated fat

0 mg cholesterol

<1 mg sodium

DIABETIC EXCHANGE:

1/2 fruit exchange

YIELD:
16 squares
(16 servings)

**PER SERVING
(1 SQUARE):**

95 calories

2 g protein

17 g carbohydrate

2 g fat

<1 g saturated fat

0 mg cholesterol

75 mg sodium

**DIABETIC
EXCHANGES:**

1/2 starch/bread
exchange

1/2 fruit exchange

Carrot Cake

1 CUP ALL-PURPOSE FLOUR

1/2 CUP LIGHT BROWN SUGAR, PACKED TO MEASURE

6 PACKETS (OR 2 TEASPOONS BULK) SWEET 'N LOW

1 TEASPOON GROUND CINNAMON

1/2 TEASPOON EACH: BAKING POWDER AND BAKING SODA

1/8 TEASPOON SALT

1/4 CUP UNSWEETENED APPLESAUCE

1/4 CUP LIQUEFIED BUTTER BUDS MIX

2 TABLESPOONS CORN OIL

2 LARGE EGG WHITES

1 TEASPOON VANILLA EXTRACT

1 CUP SHREDDED CARROTS

1/4 CUP DRIED CURRANTS OR RAISINS

2 TABLESPOONS CHOPPED WALNUTS

HONEY YOGURT CREAM, OPTIONAL (PAGE 137)

CREAM CHEESE FROSTING, OPTIONAL (PAGE 131)

Preheat the oven to 350°F. Spray an 8-inch square baking pan with nonstick cooking spray.

In a large bowl, mix the first 7 ingredients. In another bowl, combine the applesauce, Butter Buds, oil, egg whites, and vanilla. Add to the dry ingredients, stirring until well blended. Stir in the carrots, currants, and walnuts. Pour into the prepared pan. Bake 30 minutes, or until a toothpick inserted in the center comes out clean. Cool on a wire rack. Cut into 2-inch squares. Serve with Honey Yogurt Cream or Cream Cheese Frosting, if desired.

Cream Cheese Frosting

4 OUNCES NONFAT PASTEURIZED PROCESS CREAM CHEESE PRODUCT, SOFTENED

1/4 CUP REDUCED-CALORIE MARGARINE, SOFTENED

2 TABLESPOONS CONFECTIONERS' SUGAR

3 PACKETS (OR 1 TEASPOON BULK) SWEET 'N LOW

3/4 TEASPOON VANILLA EXTRACT

In a small bowl, beat all the ingredients with an electric mixer until smooth. Chill until firm.

YIELD:
3/4 cup
(12 servings)

PER SERVING (1 TABLESPOON):

35 calories

1 g protein

1 g carbohydrate

3 g fat

<1 g saturated fat

<1 mg cholesterol

75 mg sodium

DIABETIC EXCHANGE:

1/2 fat exchange

YIELD:
16 squares
(16 servings)

**PER SERVING
(1 SQUARE):**

110 calories

2 g protein

22 g carbohydrate

2 g fat

<1 g saturated fat

15 mg cholesterol

75 mg sodium

**DIABETIC
EXCHANGES:**

1 starch/bread
exchange

1/2 fruit exchange

Date-Nut Coffee Cake

Cake

1-1/4 CUPS ALL-PURPOSE FLOUR

1/4 CUP GRANULATED SUGAR

3 PACKETS (OR 1 TEASPOON BULK) SWEET 'N LOW

1 TEASPOON BAKING POWDER

1/4 TEASPOON BAKING SODA

1/8 TEASPOON SALT

1/3 CUP LIQUEFIED BUTTER BUDS MIX

1/3 CUP 1% FAT MILK

1 LARGE EGG

1 TEASPOON VANILLA EXTRACT

1 CUP CHOPPED PITTED DATES

2 TABLESPOONS CHOPPED WALNUTS

Preheat the oven to 350°F. Spray an 8-inch square baking pan with nonstick cooking spray.

In a large bowl, combine the flour, sugar, Sweet 'N Low, baking powder, baking soda, and salt. In a 1-cup measure, combine the Butter Buds, milk, egg, and vanilla. Add to the dry ingredients, stirring until blended. Add the dates and walnuts. Pour into the prepared pan.

Topping

1/4 CUP ALL-PURPOSE FLOUR

1 TABLESPOON LIGHT BROWN SUGAR, PACKED TO MEASURE

1 TABLESPOON MARGARINE, SOFTENED

1 PACKET SWEET 'N LOW

1/4 TEASPOON GROUND CINNAMON

In a small bowl, mix together all the topping ingredients until crumbly. Sprinkle over the batter. Bake 30 to 35 minutes, or until a toothpick inserted in the center comes out clean. Cool on a wire rack. Cut into 2-inch squares.

Cherry Crisp

1 CAN (20 OUNCES) REDUCED-CALORIE CHERRY PIE FILLING

1/2 CUP CRUSHED CORNFLAKES

1/4 CUP RAW QUICK-COOKING ROLLED OATS

1/4 CUP LIGHT BROWN SUGAR, PACKED TO MEASURE

2 TABLESPOONS BUTTER BUDS SPRINKLES

1 TEASPOON GROUND CINNAMON

2 TABLESPOONS REDUCED-CALORIE MARGARINE, MELTED

NONFAT FROZEN VANILLA YOGURT, OPTIONAL

Preheat the oven to 400°F. Spray an 8-inch square baking pan with nonstick cooking spray. Pour the pie filling into the pan.

In a small bowl, combine the cornflakes, oats, sugar, Butter Buds, and cinnamon; stir in the margarine. Sprinkle over the pie filling. Bake 25 to 30 minutes, or until golden brown. Cool on a wire rack. Serve with nonfat frozen vanilla yogurt, if desired.

YIELD:
6 servings

PER SERVING (1/6 CRISP WITHOUT YOGURT):

180 calories

1 g protein

40 g carbohydrate

2 g fat

<1 g saturated fat

0 mg cholesterol

195 mg sodium

DIABETIC EXCHANGES:

1-1/2 starch/bread exchanges

1 fruit exchange

Apple Pie

YIELD:
1 nine-inch pie
(8 servings)

**PER SERVING
(1/8 PIE):**

115 calories

1 g protein

29 g carbohydrate

1 g fat

<1 g saturated fat

0 mg cholesterol

65 mg sodium

**DIABETIC
EXCHANGES:**

1/2 starch/bread
exchange

1-1/2 fruit
exchanges

2 POUNDS McINTOSH APPLES, PEELED, CORED, AND THINLY
SLICED (7 CUPS)

2 TABLESPOONS LEMON JUICE

2 TABLESPOONS SUGAR

1 TABLESPOON BUTTER BUDS SPRINKLES

4 PACKETS (OR 1-1/4 TEASPOONS BULK) SWEET 'N LOW

1 TABLESPOON ALL-PURPOSE FLOUR

1-1/2 TEASPOONS GROUND CINNAMON

1/8 TEASPOON GROUND ALLSPICE

4 SHEETS PHYLLO DOUGH, THAWED

NONFAT FROZEN VANILLA YOGURT, OPTIONAL

Preheat the oven to 375°F. Spray a 9-inch pie pan with nonstick cooking spray.

In a large bowl, toss the apples with the lemon juice. In a small bowl, combine the sugar, Butter Buds, Sweet 'N Low, flour, cinnamon, and allspice. Add to the apples and toss to coat. Lightly spray one sheet of phyllo dough with nonstick cooking spray. Fold in half and spray again. Place in the pie pan with one edge hanging over the pan. Repeat the process with the remaining 3 sheets of dough, overlapping in the pan to cover the bottom completely. Spoon the apple mixture into the pan. Fold the edges of the dough over to cover the apples. Spray with nonstick cooking spray. Bake 35 minutes, or until the dough is crisp and the apples are tender when pierced with a sharp knife. Cool slightly before serving. Serve with nonfat frozen vanilla yogurt, if desired.

VARIATION: Seven cups of sliced fresh peaches or pears, or fresh blueberries, may be substituted for the apples.

Banana Cream Pie

1 GRAHAM CRACKER CRUST (PAGE 122)

1 ENVELOPE UNFLAVORED GELATIN

1/2 CUP EVAPORATED SKIM MILK

1-3/4 CUPS 1% FAT MILK

1/4 CUP SUGAR

3 PACKETS (OR 1 TEASPOON BULK) SWEET 'N LOW

1 LARGE EGG YOLK

1 TEASPOON VANILLA EXTRACT

2 MEDIUM BANANAS, PEELED AND SLICED

REDUCED-CALORIE FROZEN WHIPPED TOPPING, FOR GARNISH
(OPTIONAL)

ADDITIONAL BANANAS SLICES, FOR GARNISH (OPTIONAL)

Prepare the crust and set aside to cool.

In the top of a double boiler, soften the gelatin in the evaporated milk. In a medium bowl, combine the milk, sugar, Sweet 'N Low, and egg yolk until the yolks are well blended. Add to the double boiler. Cook over simmering water, stirring constantly, for 10 minutes, or until the mixture coats a metal spoon. Remove from the heat and stir in the vanilla. Cool slightly. Arrange the banana slices in the bottom and around the sides of the piecrust. Pour the filling over the bananas. Refrigerate several hours until firm. Garnish with the whipped topping and additional banana slices, if desired.

YIELD:
1 nine-inch pie
(8 servings)

**PER SERVING
(1/8 PIE):**

102 calories

5 g protein

30 g carbohydrate

4 g fat

1 g saturated fat

30 mg cholesterol

145 mg sodium

**DIABETIC
EXCHANGES:**

1/2 low-fat milk
exchange

1 starch/bread
exchange

1/2 fruit exchange

Brownie Sundae Pie

YIELD:
1 nine-inch pie
(8 servings)

**PER SERVING
(1/8 PIE):**

150 calories

2 g protein

28 g carbohydrate

4 g fat

1 g saturated fat

25 mg cholesterol

160 mg sodium

**DIABETIC
EXCHANGES:**

1/4 low-fat milk
exchange

1-1/2 starch/bread
exchanges

2/3 CUP SUGAR

1/4 CUP REDUCED-CALORIE MARGARINE, MELTED

1 LARGE EGG

2 TABLESPOONS BUTTER BUDS SPRINKLES

1 TEASPOON VANILLA EXTRACT

1/2 CUP ALL-PURPOSE FLOUR

1/3 CUP EUROPEAN-STYLE UNSWEETENED COCOA POWDER

1/2 TEASPOON BAKING POWDER

1/8 TEASPOON SALT

1/2 CUP REDUCED-CALORIE FROZEN WHIPPED TOPPING, THAWED

1/2 CUP SLICED BANANAS

2 TABLESPOONS CHOPPED WALNUTS

1-1/2 CUPS NONFAT VANILLA FROZEN YOGURT, OPTIONAL

Preheat the oven to 350°F. Spray a 9-inch pie pan with nonstick cooking spray.

In a large bowl, combine the sugar, margarine, egg, Butter Buds, and vanilla until well blended. Stir in the flour, cocoa, baking powder, and salt. Spread in the prepared pan. Bake 20 minutes. Cool on a wire rack. Just before serving, spoon the whipped topping decoratively around the edges of the pie. Garnish with banana slices and walnuts. Cut the pie into 8 wedges and serve with nonfat frozen vanilla yogurt, if desired.

VARIATIONS: Any sliced fresh fruit, such as strawberries, raspberries, or peaches, may be used in place of the sliced bananas.

Omit the whipped topping, bananas, and walnuts; serve with nonfat frozen vanilla yogurt and Raspberry Sauce (page 128) or Strawberry Sauce (page 129).

Honey Yogurt Cream

1 CUP YOGURT CHEESE (PAGE 53)

1 TABLESPOON HONEY

2 TO 3 PACKETS SWEET 'N LOW

In a small container, combine the Yogurt Cheese and honey. Stir in enough Sweet 'N Low to achieve the desired sweetness. Serve with Fresh Fruit Kabobs (page 40).

NOTE: To use as a dressing for fruit salad, thin with 2 to 3 tablespoons of unsweetened fruit juice, such as apple, orange, or pure fruit juice blends.

YIELD:
1 cup (8 servings)

PER SERVING (2 TABLESPOONS):

40 calories

3 g protein

7 g carbohydrate

0 g fat

0 g saturated fat

<1 mg cholesterol

40 mg sodium

DIABETIC EXCHANGE:

1/2 nonfat milk exchange

Beverages

If you're looking for a mug of warm Mulled Cider on a cold winter's night, a Tropical Shake for Two for a romantic interlude, or a light Apple-Raspberry Spritzer for a low-calorie treat—we've got what you're looking for. Fruits, spices, and exciting flavor combinations make these beverages a special treat.

Cranberry-Orange Iced Tea

YIELD:
6 cups (6 servings)

**PER SERVING
(1 CUP):**

40 calories

<1 g protein

9 g carbohydrate

<1 g fat

<1 g saturated fat

0 mg cholesterol

10 mg sodium

**DIABETIC
EXCHANGE:**

1/2 fruit exchange

2 CUPS BOILING WATER

6 CRANBERRY HERB TEA BAGS

1/4 CUP LEMON JUICE

9 PACKETS (OR 1 TABLESPOON BULK) SWEET 'N LOW

2-1/2 CUPS COLD WATER

1-1/2 CUPS ORANGE JUICE

In a large pitcher, pour the boiling water over the tea bags. Steep 5 minutes; remove the tea bags and discard. Stir in the lemon juice and Sweet 'N Low until the Sweet 'N Low dissolves. Mix in the cold water and orange juice. Refrigerate until well chilled. Pour over ice in tall glasses.

Apple-Raspberry Spritzer

1 CUP BOILING WATER
2 APPLE-CINNAMON HERB TEA BAGS
2 CUPS BOTTLED UNSWEETENED RASPBERRY JUICE BLEND
2 TABLESPOONS LEMON JUICE
3 PACKETS (OR 1 TEASPOON BULK) SWEET 'N LOW
2 CUPS COLD CLUB SODA

In a large pitcher, pour the boiling water over the tea bags. Steep 10 minutes; remove the tea bags and discard. Stir in the raspberry juice, lemon juice, and Sweet 'N Low. Refrigerate until well chilled. Just before serving, mix in the club soda.

TIP: Be aware of the "hidden" sugar content in many flavored bottled waters and "natural" sodas.

YIELD:
5 cups (5 servings)

PER SERVING (1 CUP):
40 calories
<1 g protein
9 g carbohydrate
<1 g fat
<1 g saturated fat
0 mg cholesterol
30 mg sodium

DIABETIC EXCHANGE:
1/2 fruit exchange

Breakfast Shake

YIELD:
1-1/2 cups
(1 serving)

**PER SERVING
(1-1/2 CUPS):**

220 calories

10 g protein

42 g carbohydrate

1 g fat

<1 g saturated fat

<1 mg cholesterol

110 mg sodium

**DIABETIC
EXCHANGES:**

1 nonfat milk
exchange

1 starch/bread
exchange

1 fruit exchange

1/2 CUP LOW-FAT VANILLA YOGURT

1/4 CUP SKIM MILK

2 TABLESPOONS FROZEN ORANGE JUICE CONCENTRATE

1 TABLESPOON WHEAT GERM

2 PACKETS SWEET 'N LOW

1/2 TEASPOON VANILLA EXTRACT

3 ICE CUBES

In a blender at medium speed, blend all the ingredients until smooth and frothy. Pour into a glass.

VARIATION: Add 1/2 cup sliced bananas; blend as directed.

Tropical Shake for Two

1/2 CUP LOW-FAT VANILLA YOGURT

1/2 CUP SLICED BANANA

1/4 CUP CRUSHED PINEAPPLE PACKED IN UNSWEETENED JUICE

1/4 CUP SKIM MILK

2 PACKETS SWEET 'N LOW

1/2 TEASPOON COCONUT EXTRACT

6 ICE CUBES

In a blender at medium speed, blend all the ingredients until smooth and frothy. Pour into 2 glasses.

YIELD:
2 cups (2 servings)

PER SERVING (1 CUP):

130 calories

4 g protein

29 g carbohydrate

<1 g fat

<1 g saturated fat

<1 mg cholesterol

55 mg sodium

DIABETIC EXCHANGES:

1/2 nonfat milk exchange

1-1/2 fruit exchanges

YIELD:
1-1/2 cups (1 serving)

PER SERVING (1-1/2 CUPS):

135 calories

9 g protein

25 g carbohydrate

<1 g fat

0 g saturated fat

5 mg cholesterol

120 mg sodium

DIABETIC EXCHANGES:

1 nonfat milk exchange

1 fruit exchange

Smooth Strawberry Shake

3/4 CUP FROZEN UNSWEETENED STRAWBERRIES

1/2 CUP PLAIN NONFAT YOGURT

1/4 CUP SKIM MILK

1 ICE CUBE

1/2 TEASPOON VANILLA EXTRACT

1 TO 2 PACKETS SWEET 'N LOW

In a blender at medium speed, blend all the ingredients until smooth and frothy. Pour into a glass.

TIP: Did you know that strawberries are a good source of vitamin C?

Perfectly Peach Shake

Substitute *3/4 cup frozen sliced peaches* for the strawberries; increase the *vanilla* to *1 teaspoon*; use *2 packets Sweet 'N Low*.

YIELD:
1-1/2 cups
(1 serving)

**PER SERVING
(1-1/2 CUPS):**

160 calories

9 g protein

29 g carbohydrate

<1 g fat

0 g saturated fat

5 mg cholesterol

120 mg sodium

**DIABETIC
EXCHANGES:**

1 nonfat milk
exchange

1 fruit exchange

YIELD:
1-1/2 cups
(1 serving)

**PER SERVING
(1-1/2 CUPS):**

180 calories

9 g protein

35 g carbohydrate

<1 g fat

0 g saturated fat

5 mg cholesterol

120 mg sodium

**DIABETIC
EXCHANGES:**

1 nonfat milk
exchange

1-1/2 fruit
exchanges

Peach Melba Shake

Substitute *1/2 cup frozen sliced peaches* and *1/4 cup frozen raspberries* for the strawberries. Increase the *vanilla* to *1 teaspoon*; use 2 packets Sweet 'N Low.

Mulled Cider

1 QUART APPLE CIDER OR APPLE JUICE

1/2 CUP WATER

5 WHOLE CLOVES

5 CINNAMON STICKS

3 PACKETS (OR 1 TEASPOON BULK) SWEET 'N LOW

1/4 TEASPOON EACH: GROUND GINGER AND GROUND NUTMEG

In a large saucepan over medium heat, bring all the ingredients to a boil. Reduce the heat and simmer 20 minutes. Strain the mixture, reserving the cinnamon sticks. Place 1 cinnamon stick in each of 5 mugs and pour 3/4 cup hot cider into each mug.

YIELD:
3-3/4 cups
(5 servings)

**PER SERVING
(3/4 CUP):**

105 calories

< 1 g protein

28 g carbohydrate

< 1 g fat

0 mg saturated fat

0 mg cholesterol

10 mg sodium

**DIABETIC
EXCHANGES:**

2 fruit exchanges

YIELD:
1 cup (1 serving)

**PER SERVING
(1 CUP):**

95 calories

9 g protein

14 g carbohydrate

<1 g fat

<1 g saturated fat

5 mg cholesterol

130 mg sodium

**DIABETIC
EXCHANGE:**

1 nonfat milk
exchange

Café au Lait

1 CUP SKIM MILK

1 PACKET SWEET 'N LOW

1/4 TEASPOON GROUND CINNAMON

**1 TEASPOON INSTANT COFFEE GRANULES,
REGULAR OR DECAFFEINATED**

In a small saucepan over medium-low heat, heat the milk, Sweet 'N Low, and cinnamon mixture until it simmers. Place the coffee granules in a mug; add the hot milk and stir until blended.

Menus for All Occasions

A Western Barbecue theme for a family
gathering, a Romantic Retreat to put the spark
back into your relationship, a Holiday Dinner
for Thanksgiving, Christmas, or Chanukah, a
Best Ever Brunch for your favorite birthday
person—we've prepared menu suggestions for
the special occasions in your life. Use your
imagination to give a personal touch to
these menus.

For a birthday, Mother's Day, Father's Day, or any other special occasion, there's nothing better than enjoying a late-morning brunch with your favorite people! Served on a pretty tray with flowers, it's one wake-up call that won't be forgotten.

Best Ever Brunch

Orange Juice Spritzers

Spanish Potato Omelet
page 41

Assorted Muffins
pages 34-37

Fresh Fruit Salad

Café au Lait
page 148

While the Super Bowl comes but once a year, these winning snacks are sure to be a hit when watching any of your favorite sporting events! Get everyone into the spirit by providing guests with pom-poms and encouraging them to make signs for cheering on their teams. In addition, some of these dishes can also be taken on the road to the game. Salsa, popcorn, cookies, and cider all travel well.

Winning Super Bowl Snacks

Potato Skins with Variations
pages 44-46

Broccoli-Ricotta Pizza
page 63

Chicken Fingers with Horseradish Dip
pages 47, 96

Garden Fresh Salsa with Pita Crisps
pages 49, 51

Air-Popped Popcorn Seasoned with Butter Buds Sprinkles

Oatmeal Raisin Cookies
page 116

Mulled Cider
pages 147

Whether it's a business gathering or a friendly get-together, your guests won't stop raving about the fabulous caterer for this cocktail party. Shhhh—you don't have to tell them it was you!

Cocktail Party

Garlic Stuffed Mushrooms
page 79

Couscous Salad Stuffed Vegetables
page 71

Spicy Shrimp
page 48

Ratatouille over Cooked Pasta Shells
page 76

Assorted Crudités with Crabmeat Dip
page 50

Cranberry-Orange Iced Tea
page 140

Everyone loves a good barbecue. This western barbecue is not only easy to prepare but delicious! Wear a cowboy hat, use red-and-white checked tablecloths, and serve with big Texas-size plates and cups to bring the good old West into your backyard.

Western Barbecue

Flank Steak in Teriyaki Marinade
page 87

Barbecued Chicken with Barbecue Sauce
page 83

Mixed Vegetable Slaw
page 72

Crunchy Potato Salad
page 70

Corn on the Cob with Liquefied Butter Buds Mix

Cherry Crisp
page 133

Going on a picnic is a great way to get fresh air and spend time with your family and friends. This perfect picnic is a healthy feast that will tantilize your taste buds. Pack it in a wicker picnic basket and spread it onto a large blanket under a tree for the perfect finishing touches.

Perfect Picnic

Rosemary Roasted Chicken Breasts
page 98

Tortellini Salad
page 69

Dilled Cucumbers
page 77

Mini Rolls

Banana Spice Cake
page 124

Apple-Raspberry Spritzer
page 141

Whether you've just gotten engaged, are celebrating an anniversary, or have just put the kids to bed, this romantic retreat will set the mood for a memorable evening. Light candles, set the table with your good china, and put on your favorite music to make it even more special.

Romantic Retreat

Cream of Fresh Tomato Soup
page 66

Pita Crisps
page 49

Mixed Salad with Herb Vinaigrette
page 89

Saffron Scallops with Angel Hair Pasta
page 109-110

Creamy Chocolate Pudding (served in individual glasses
and garnished with fruit)
page 121

Almond Cookies
page 118

Holidays were meant for celebrating. And what better way to enjoy the festivities than with a healthy—yet hearty—holiday dinner!

Holiday Dinner

Honey-Citrus Glazed Turkey Breast
page 105

Herb Stuffing
page 80

Gingered Carrots and Snow Peas
page 74

Fresh Steamed Green Beans

Hot Apple Pie
page 134

Fat-Free Frozen Yogurt

Harvest Pumpkin Squares
page 123

Café au Lait
page 148

Conversions

Equivalent Imperial and Metric Measurements

American cooks use standard containers, the 8-ounce cup and a tablespoon that takes exactly 16 level fillings to fill that cup level. Measuring by cup makes it very difficult to give weight equivalents, as a cup of densely packed butter will weigh considerably more than a cup of flour. The easiest way therefore to deal with cup measurements in recipes is to take the amount by volume rather than by weight. Thus the equation reads:

$$1 \text{ cup} = 240 \text{ ml} = 8 \text{ fl. oz.} \qquad 1/2 \text{ cup} = 120 \text{ ml} = 4 \text{ fl. oz.}$$

It is possible to buy a set of American cup measures in major stores around the world.

In the States, butter is often measured in sticks. One stick is the equivalent of 8 tablespoons. One tablespoon of butter is therefore the equivalent of 1/2 ounce/14 grams.

Liquid Measures

FLUID OUNCES	U.S. MEASURES	IMPERIAL MEASURES	MILLILITERS
	1 tsp	1 tsp	5
	2 tsp	1 dessertspoon	10
1/2	1 tbs	1 tbs	14
1	2 tbs	2 tbs	28
2	1/4 cup	4 tbs	56
4	1/2 cup		110
5		1/4 pint or 1 gill	140
6	3/4 cup		170
8	1 cup		225
9			250 or 1/4 liter
10	1-1/4 cups	1/2 pint	280
12	1-1/2 cups		340
15		3/4 pint	420

16	2 cups		450
18	2-1/4 cups		500 or 1/2 liter
20	2-1/2 cups	1 pint	560
24	3 cups		675
25		1-1/4 pints	700
27	3-1/2 cups		750
30	3-3/4 cups	1-1/2 pints	840
32	4 cups or 1 quart		900
35		1-3/4 pints	980
36	4-1/2 cups		1000 or 1 liter
40	5 cups	2 pints or 1 quart	1120
48	6 cups		1350
50		2-1/2 pints	1400
60	7-1/2 cups	3 pints	1680
64	8 cups or 2 quarts		1800
72	9 cups		2000 or 2 liters
80	10 cups	4 pints	2250
96	12 cups or 3 quarts		2700
100		5 pints	2800

Solid Measures

U.S. AND IMPERIAL MEASURES		METRIC MEASURES	
OUNCES	**POUNDS**	**GRAMS**	**KILOS**
1		28	
2		56	
3-1/2		100	
4	1/4	112	
5		140	
6		168	
8	1/2	225	
9		250	1/4
12	3/4	340	
16	1	450	
18		500	1/2
20	1-1/4	560	
24	1-1/2	675	
27		750	3/4
28	1-3/4	780	
32	2	900	
36	2-1/4	1000	1
40	2-1/2	1100	
48	3	1350	
54		1500	1-1/2
64	4	1800	
72	4-1/2	2000	2
80	5	2250	2-1/4
90		2500	2-1/2
100	6	2800	2-3/4

Oven Temperature Equivalents

FAHRENHEIT	CELSIUS	GAS MARK	DESCRIPTION
225	110	1/4	Cool
250	130	1/2	
275	140	1	Very Slow
300	150	2	
325	170	3	Slow
350	180	4	Moderate
375	190	5	
400	200	6	Moderately Hot
425	220	7	Fairly Hot
450	230	8	Hot
475	240	9	Very Hot
500	250	10	Extremely Hot

Any broiling recipes can be used with the oven grill, but beware of high-temperature grills.

Index

Recipes Grouped by Products